The York Mystery Plays

in a new version by Mike Poulton

This version of *The York Mystery Plays* was
first performed at York Minster on 26 May 2016

Author's Note
Mike Poulton

Twenty years ago the director David Hunt asked me to turn the middle-English poem *St Erkenwald* into a play for the RSC's medieval season in The Other Place. This involved creating dialogue for a cross-section of the people of fifteenth-century London – knights, scholars, bishops, workers, saints and jokers – and then translating it into the words and rhythms of the period. I became hooked on the language of the fourteenth and fifteenth centuries. It was probably because of the success of *St Erkenwald* that Greg Doran asked me to edit and adapt the *York Mysteries* for the production he'd been asked to direct, with David, in the Minster, as part of York's Millennium celebrations. I couldn't have been more delighted, and began to immerse myself in the language and culture of the medieval city.

The scope and completeness of the York cycle is astonishing. The subtlety and variety of the verse and characterisation are accessible and actable. Today the vocabulary may have changed but the old rhythms are detectable still in the Yorkshire dialect. On setting to work it became clear to me that the text is the work of playwrights rather than authors – people who understood how a play works, and knew how to write clear and deliverable lines, as well as when to stand back from the script and leave everything to the director and the actors. So my approach to the text was to retain as much of the original as I thought would be accessible to today's audience. As far as possible I kept the original words, rhythms, and speech patterns. Where I had to modernise I attempted to show the spirit that lies under the lines rather than produce a prosaic translation of the lines themselves. And most of all I tried to offer each character in the play the personality and individuality I found in the original text. So I hope my version has the right mix of humour, joy, pathos, and grandeur that make the original *York Mysteries* one of the great achievements of European literature.

The first production of the plays in the Minster, commissioned by the Dean, Ray Furnell, was seen by nearly 30,000 people, and so successful that we immediately began discussions for a new production 'in the near future'. Sixteen years later we are back with a new Dean and the same enthusiasm and spirit of adventure that characterised the first undertaking. When the plays were first performed in the streets of the city, the vaulting of the Nave of the Minster had just been completed, the old Norman parts of the building were being demolished and rebuilt, and the central tower was on the point of collapse. Since then restoration work has been ongoing. The great East Window, restored at a cost of many millions, should be revealed in its pristine glory next year. The plays are as much a part of the community and fabric of York as the Minster itself.

But words, like windows age and grow tarnished and – just as the glass and stonework of the building has to be constantly repaired and maintained – I felt that my original text would benefit from a thorough overhaul. So the text we are using in the current production is, I hope, new and vibrant. I've tried to give the actors lines they'll relish delivering, and the audience an enjoyable and uplifting experience in one of the finest buildings in the western world.

The Mystery in the Minster

Since the 1300s, the *York Mystery Plays* have entertained residents and visitors to the city of York, bringing to life the greatest story ever told. For only the second time in their near seven-hundred-year history, the *Plays* returned to York Minster for a breathtaking production of the city's most famous stories in its most iconic building.

The medieval Minster's magnificent Nave transformed into a 1,000-seater auditorium for the production, which opened on Thursday 26 May – the feast of Corpus Christi – and ran for five weeks and 41 performances until Thursday 30 June.

In keeping with tradition, the vast community cast featured just one paid actor, and the production was supported by an army of backstage volunteers to create a unique spectacle, which celebrated the city's cultural heritage.

The production aimed to provoke tears and laughter and be an intensely moving experience, but above all offered a once-in-a-generation opportunity to see the city's most famous stories brought to life in its most iconic building.

York Minster is one of the world's most magnificent cathedrals – a masterpiece in stained glass and stone with foundations rooted in the nation's earliest history. The current building is around eight hundred years old and is at least the second Minster to stand in the location, but the history of the site actually dates back more than 2,000 years.

Some of the earliest records of the *Mystery Plays* date from the 1300s, so parts of the Minster which we see today would have been in existence at the time they were performed. The Minster is the largest medieval Gothic cathedral in northern Europe and more than half of England's medieval stained glass is held in its one hundred and twenty-eight windows. The Great East Window is the single largest expanse of medieval stained glass in the country. The Old Testament panels are housed within the window and tell the stories dramatised in the *Mystery Plays*.

The Nave, the setting for the *Mystery Plays*, is one of the longest in England at a staggering 80m long and 30m wide, with the ornate vaulted ceiling towering 29m above the floor. The Nave has only been used for services since 1863 and in recent years has hosted a range of concerts and events, including the acclaimed production of the *Mystery Plays* in 2000.

Today as a working cathedral, York Minster welcomes visitors from around the world to share in daily life and worship, to explore the past and to enjoy a busy programme of events and concerts.

Biographies

Mike Poulton (Writer)

Mike Poulton is an English writer, translator and adapter of classic plays for contemporary audiences. He began writing for the theatre in 1995. His first two productions were staged the following year at the Chichester Festival Theatre: *Uncle Vanya* with Derek Jacobi, and *Fortune's Fool* with Alan Bates.

In 2000 Mike wrote the *York Millennium Mystery Plays* staged at York Minster. His work has been performed in theatres throughout Britain and Ireland, in London's West End, and on Broadway, throughout Europe and at the Royal Shakespeare Company, Chichester Festival Theatre, Clwyd Theatr Cymru, the West Yorkshire Playhouse, the Crucible Sheffield, the Mercury Theatre Colchester, the Theatre Royal Bath, the Theatre Royal Northampton, the Old Vic, the Almeida, and the Donmar Warehouse. He is currently under contract to the RSC.

Notably, in 2005 his adaptation of Schiller's *Don Carlos* (Crucible, Sheffield and West End), with Derek Jacobi and directed by Michael Grandage, won an Olivier Award. In 2003 his *Fortune's Fool*, directed by Arthur Penn on Broadway, received a Tony nomination for Best Play and went on to win seven major awards including the Tony for Best Actor for Alan Bates, and the Tony for Best Featured Actor for Frank Langella.

Recently, Mike wrote the scripts for the RSC's productions of Hilary Mantel's global best-selling novels *Wolf Hall* and *Bring Up the Bodies*. The production became a sensation for the RSC in 2013–2014, breaking box-office records at Stratford-upon-Avon and at the Aldwych in London.

The RSC's production played for four months on the American stage on Broadway and in April 2015 was nominated for eight Tony awards.

Phillip Breen (Director)

Phillip studied at Cambridge University and trained at Clwyd Theatr Cymru under Terry Hands after winning a RYTDS Bursary.

Directing credits include *Lady Chatterley's Lover* (Sheffield Crucible/ETT); *Cyrano de Bergerac*, *The Birthday Party*, *Suddenly Last Summer*, *Measure for Measure*, *Two Princes* by Meredydd Barker, *Cariad* by Sophie Stanton (Clwyd Theatr Cymru); *Orpheus Descending* (Theatre Cocoon, Tokyo – Yomiura Award Nomination); *The Shoemaker's Holiday* (RSC); *True West* (Citizens, Glasgow/Tricycle, London; Digital Theatre, British Theatre Award nomination); *Holes* by Tom Basden (Arcola Tent); *The Merry Wives of Windsor* (RSC); *Threeway* by DC Jackson (Edinburgh, Invisible Dot); Vivienne Westwood's Alternative Christmas Lecture (RSC at Wilton's Music Hall); *Sex With a Stranger* by Stefan Golaszewski (Trafalgar Studios); *A Day in the Death of Joe Egg*, *The Resistible Rise of Arturo Ui*, *The Shadow of a Gunman*, *The Caretaker* (Citizens, Glasgow); *Dumb Show* (New Vic, Stoke); *Party* by Tom Basden (Edinburgh, West End, Sydney International Theatre Festival, West End – Fringe First Winner); *The Stefan Golaszewski Plays* (Traverse, Edinburgh/Bush, London/ Off-Broadway; Fringe First winner); *Dymock Watson: Nazi Smasher* (Edinburgh, West End, UCB, Los Angeles; Edinburgh Comedy Award winner); *The Hard Man* by Jimmy Boyle and Tom McGrath (Scottish Touring Consortium; CATS Award nomination).

Writing credits include an adaptation of *Lady Chatterley's Lover* (Sheffield Crucible/ETT); *The Resistible Rise of Arturo Ui* (Citizens, Glasgow); *Crime and Punishment* (LAMDA); *Director's Shakespeare* and *Actor's Shakespeare*, published by Routledge.

Max Jones (Designer)

Max Jones is a London-based theatre designer who has designed productions across the UK and internationally, including for Shakespeare's Globe, the Royal Shakespeare Company, Theatre Cocoon Tokyo and Clwyd Theatr Cymru, where he is an Associate Artist. Max has worked also extensively as a costume assistant for major feature films.

Max graduated from the Royal Welsh College of Music and Drama in 2001 and during that year was one of four people to win the Linbury Biennial Prize for Stage Design. He was recently nominated in the Best Design category at the 2014 UK Theatre Awards for the *True West* production at the Citizens Theatre, Glasgow.

Recent productions include *The Crucible* (Royal Exchange Theatre, Manchester); *The Broken Heart, The Tempest* (Shakespeare's Globe); *Orpheus Descending* (Japan); *Queen Coal* (Sheffield Crucible); *The Shoemaker's Holiday, The Merry Wives of Windsor* (RSC); *Pride and Prejudice* (Regent's Park Open Air) and *Of Mice and Men* (West Yorkshire Playhouse).

Richard Shephard (Music Director)

Richard Shephard is acclaimed as one of the most significant composers of church music today. He is Visiting Fellow in the Department of Music at York University and a member of the University's Court.

He was formerly Headmaster of the Minster School in York from 1985–2004 and served as Chamberlain of York Minster and Director of Development for the York Minster Fund, responsible for raising funding for restoration and conservation work at the cathedral.

He has served on the Archbishops' Commission on Church Music and on cathedrals and was also visiting Professor in the Music Department of the University of the South, Sewanee, Tennessee. He holds a number of honorary doctorates in music, as well as an Honorary Fellowship of the Royal School of Church Music.

In collaboration with American musician and composer Mark Schweizer, Richard has written a number of operas. His work also includes a number of light operettas, musicals, orchestral works, music for television, and chamber music but he is perhaps best known for his choral works which are sung extensively around the world today, especially in churches and cathedrals in England and America. His compositions are frequently broadcast in the United Kingdom.

He was appointed MBE in the 2012 Queen's Birthday Honours list for his services to music and education and is an Honorary Freeman of the City of York.

Ayse Tashkiran (Movement Director)
Ayse Tashkiran is a movement director and performer. After completing a degree in drama at Bristol University she trained at L'École International Jacques Lecoq in Paris from 1990 to 1992.

Current movement direction includes *Dr Faustus* by Christopher Marlowe, direction by Maria Aberg for Royal Shakespeare Company in The Swan, and *The Government Inspector* by Nikolai Gogol, directed by Roxana Silbert at Birmingham Repertory Theatre and national tour.

Recent work includes *Barbarians* (Young Vic); *Hecuba*, *The White Devil*, *The Shoemaker's Holiday*, *As You Like It*, *The Merry Wives of Windsor*, *King John*, *Richard III* and *Measure for Measure* (RSC); *Shh…Bang!* (Peut-Être); *The Sleeper* (Welsh National Opera); *Little Eagles* (RSC at the Hampstead); *The Chairs* (Theatre Royal Bath); *Day of Significance* (RSC, tour) and *Sweeney Todd* (Welsh National Opera MAX).

Liam Evans-Ford (Fight Director)
Liam began his stage-combat training at Bristol Old Vic Theatre School under the tutorship of fight director Jonathan Howell. He continued his training at the Royal Shakespeare Company.

Fight directing credits include *Guys and Dolls* (Palace, Manchester); *West Side Story* (RSG at The Harlequin); *Boiling Frogs* (The Factory at Southwark Playhouse); *I Caught Crabs in Walberswick* (HighTide Festival/Bush); *Macbeth*, *Romeo and Juliet*, *The Tempest*, *Twelfth Night*, *A Midsummer Night's Dream* (Sprite Productions); *The Crucible, Peter Pan, Blackbird* (York Theatre Royal, In The Round Ensemble Season); *Loneliness of the Long Distance Runner, Antigone, Blood & Chocolate* and *Blackbird* (Pilot); *iShandy, Robin Hood and His Merry Mam!, The Legend of King Arthur, See How They Run, The Guinea Pig Club, In Fog and Falling Snow, York Mystery Plays 2012, Helver's Night, The Wind in the Willows* (York Theatre Royal); *Aladdin, Neville's Island* (Stephen Joseph); *Oliver!, Dick Whittington, Show Boat* (Sheffield Theatres); *Camelot: The Shining City* (Slung Low, Sheffield Theatres); *The White Whale* (Slung Low); *Inkheart* (HOME, Manchester); *Robin Hood* (Leeds City Varieties); *Sleeping Beauty* (CAST); *Show Boat* (New London). Liam is an associate fight director at Pendley Shakespeare Festival where he has choreographed fights on productions such as *Macbeth*, *Hamlet, Romeo and Juliet, The Comedy of Errors* and *King Lear*.

Becky Hope-Palmer (Associate Director)
Becky trained at the Royal Conservatoire of Scotland. Her credits as a director include *The Hen Night, Like a Moth to a Flame* (Royal Conservatoire of Scotland); *The Winter's Tale* (Royal Conservatoire of Scotland in association with Shakespeare's Globe); *It Never Ends* (Cumbernauld/Traverse); *The Cameo* (A Play, a Pie and a Pint at Oràn Mór); *Buffer, Riot Squat* (Thrive).

Her Assistant Director credits include *Tomorrow* (Vanishing Point); *Kill Johnny Glendenning, Bondagers, Faith Healer, Hedda Gabler, The Venetian Twins, Union* (Lyceum, Edinburgh).

She is also the founder and Artistic Director of Edinburgh-based company, Thrive Theatre.

Ruth Hall (Associate Designer)
Ruth Hall is a London-based freelance set and costume designer for theatre in the UK and abroad. She trained at the Royal Welsh College of Music and Drama, achieving a first-class BA Hons in Theatre Design. Following graduation, she was selected as a Trainee Designer to join the Royal Shakespeare Company's apprenticeship programme 2005-6. Recently she has received nominations in best design from the Welsh Critics Awards for *Salt, Root and Roe* (Clwyd Theatr Cymru), and *Y Fenyw Ddaeth o'r Môr* (Theatr Genedlaethol Cymru).

Recent design credits include *Little Shop of Horrors, Sky Hawk, Salt, Root and Roe* (Clwyd Theatr Cymru); *Y Fenyw Ddaeth o'r Môr* (Theatr Genedlaethol Cymru); *Blasted* (The Other Room); *Play Strindberg* (Ustinov, Bath); *Contractions* (Chapter Arts Centre); *Fijiland*, (Southwark Playhouse); *Altogether Now*, a devised adaptation (North Wall and Awake Projects, youth-outreach project, Oxford).

Art Department Assistant on *London Road* (film) Cuba Pictures, 2014.

Associate Designer on *Orpheus Descending* (Theatre Cocoon, Tokyo); *Of Mice and Men* (West Yorkshire Playhouse) and *Crime and Punishment* (Citizens, Glasgow).

Tina MacHugh (Lighting Designer)
Theatre credits include *The Merry Wives of Windsor, The Shoemaker's Holiday, The Tempest, The Comedy of Errors, The Phoenician Women, Shadows* and *Ghosts* (Olivier Award nomination, all RSC); *The Machine Wreckers, Guiding Star* and *Rutherford and Son* (Olivier Award nomination, all National Theatre); *True West, The Caretaker* (Citizens, Glasgow); *Dumb Show* (New Vic, Stoke); *Cyrano de Bergerac, Measure for Measure, The Grapes of Wrath* (Clwyd Theatr Cymru); *The Recruiting Officer, The Alice Trilogy* (Abbey, Dublin); *Paradise Bound* (Liverpool Everyman); *Mrs Pat* (York Theatre Royal); *When Harry Met Sally* (UK tour); *Book of Evidence* (Gate, Dublin; Irish Times Best Lighting Design nomination); *Nixon's Nixon* (West End/Australian tour); *A Doll's House, Spoonface Steinberg, Mother Courage* (West End); *Sweeney Todd* (Derby Playhouse); *Midden* (Hampstead); *Our Father* (Almeida); *Yard Gal, Live Like Pigs* (Royal Court); *The Wexford Trilogy* (Bush).

Opera includes *Idomeneo* for LA Opera with Placido Domingo, *Orlando, Apollo and Hyacinthus, Pelleas and Melisande* (OTC Dublin); *The Turn of the Screw* (Wilton's Music Hall); *Der Rosenkavalier* (Scottish Opera); *Il re pastore* (Opera North); *La bohème, A Streetcar Named Desire* (Opera Ireland) and *Alcina, Falstaff* (ETO).

Dance credits include Geneva Ballet, Houston Ballet, Royal Danish Ballet, London Contemporary Dance Theatre, DV8, Adventures in Motion Pictures, English National Ballet, and Rambert Dance Company.

Andrea J Cox (Sound Designer)
Studied Physics and Philosophy at Liverpool University. She has designed shows and worked for the Liverpool Everyman Theatre, Bristol Old Vic and most extensively for the Royal Shakespeare Company.

Recent theatre sound designs include *The Patriotic Traitor* (Finsbury); *Harvest* (Bath/Soho); *Jekyll & Hyde* (UK tour); *The Shoemaker's Holiday* (RSC); *Play Strindberg* (Bath); *True West* (Tricycle/Citizens, Glasgow); *Holes* (Arcola/Edinburgh); *The Big Meal* (Bath/HighTide Festival); *Alarms and Excursions* (Chipping Norton); *Threeway* (Edinburgh Fringe); *Charlotte's Web* (Derby); *Sex With a Stranger* (Trafalgar Studios); *Yes, Prime Minister* (Chichester/West End/LA); *Onassis* (Derby/West End); *Calendar Girls* (Chichester/tour); *Pieces* (Clwyd/New York); *The Oresteia Trilogy* (Fisher Center, New York); *Sons of York* (Finborough); *The Pull of Negative Gravity* (Colchester/Edinburgh/New York).

Over fifty sound designs for the RSC, including *The Histories* (all eight plays from *Richard II* to *Richard III*), *Twelfth Night*, *The Winter's Tale*, *Measure for Measure*, *Macbeth*, *Hamlet*, *The Comedy of Errors*, *Troilus and Cressida*, *Theban Plays*, *Elgar's Rondo*, *Little Eyolf*, *Tales From Ovid*, *Henry VI's* and *Richard III* (Michigan, USA/Young Vic), *As You Like It* (Washington DC), *Ghosts*, *The Phoenician Women*, *The Mysteries*, *Shadows*, *Bad Weather*, *A Warwickshire Testimony*.

Douglas O'Connell (Video Designer)
Douglas is both a designer as well as the leading educator in the UK in video design for performance.

Recent video design credits include *Into the Woods* (West Yorkshire Playhouse); *Don Giovanni* (Hampstead Garden Opera); *Mozart and Son: Benefit Gala* (Royal Opera House); *300th Anniversary St John's Smith Square, The Five O'Clock Slot* (Ice & Fire); *Fault Lines* (Hampstead); *Letter of Last Resort* (Traverse); *Sticks and Stones* (Polka); *The Bomb* (Tricycle); *Dance Marathon* (Barbican); *Fit and Proper People* (RSC/Soho); *Silence* (RSC/Filter); *Behud* (Coventry); *Monsters* (Arcola); *This Isn't Romance* (Soho); *50th Anniversary Gala of Harold Pinter's The Birthday Party, Fight Face, Sarajevo Story* (Lyric, Hammersmith); *Saturday Night Sunday Morning* (Harrogate); *Here's What I Did with My Body One Day* (national tour).

Upcoming work includes *Pinocchio* (Toronto National Ballet).

Philip McGinley (Lead Actor, Jesus)
Television credits include *Home Fires*, *No Offence*, *Drifters*, *Game of Thrones*, *The Gemma Factor*, *Coronation Street*, *Cold Blood*, *Blue Murder*, *Heartbeat*, *Casualty*, *The Bill*, *Falling*, *The Deputy*, *Dalziel & Pascoe*.

Theatre credits include *Husbands & Sons* (National Theatre/Royal Exchange Theatre, Manchester); *The Daughter-in-Law*, *Hobson's Choice* (Sheffield Crucible); *Straight* (Sheffield Studio/Bush); *Herding Cats* (Hampstead/Ustinov, Bath); *Canary* (ETT/Liverpool Playhouse/Hampstead); *More Light* (Arcola); *The Changeling* (Cheek by Jowl); *Great Expectations* (RSC) and *Kes* (Royal Exchange Theatre, Manchester).

Film credits include *Almost Married*, *Prometheus* and *Molehills*.

Creatives

Written by **Mike Poulton**
Directed by **Phillip Breen**
   with **Becky Hope-Palmer**
Designed by **Max Jones**
   with **Ruth Hall**
Music Director
   Richard Shephard
Movement Director **Ayse Tashkiran**
Fight Director **Liam Evans-Ford**
Lighting Designer **Tina MacHugh**
Chief LX **Adam Povey**
Sound Designer **Andrea J Cox**
Head of Sound **Ken Hampton**
Video Designer **Douglas O'Connell**
Design Assistant **Ella Callow**
Technical Support **Alan Bartlett**
Movement Placement **Patricia Verity**
Producer **Nicola Corp**
Production Manager
   Joan Humphreys
Technical Production Manager
   Paul Veysey
Production Coordinator
   Stephanie O'Gorman
Production Support **Laura Cookson**
Stage Manager **John Pemberton**
Assistant Stage Manager
   Emily Humphreys
Assistant Stage Manager (rehearsals)
   Robert Perkins
Assistant Stage Manager
   Sophie Robyn
Assistant Stage Manager
   Rosie Ward
Technical Assistant Stage Manager
   Paul Veysey
Assistant to Musical Director
   Connor McLean
Assistant to Musical Director
   Danny Purtell
Props Supervisor **Beckie May**
Props Assistant **Scott Thompson**
Props Assistant **Mark Kesteven**
Props Assistant **Donna Taylor**
Props Assistant **Anna Kesteven**

Props Assistant
   Catharina Golebiowska
Props Assistant **Paul Lazenby**
Scenic Painters **Rory Davis**
Scenic Painters **Anna Roberts**
Scenic Painters **Christine Bradnum**
Scenic Painters **Frances Connor**
Scenic Painters **Matt Grace**
Scenic Painters **Sarah Grace**
Costume Co-Supervisor
   Fiona Parker
Costume Co-Supervisor
   Lorraine Ebdon
Costume painter/distresser
   Janet Spriggs
Workshop Supervisor **Fran Brammer**
Workshop Supervisor **Kelly Reagon**
Wardrobe Mistress
   Sarah Colebourne-Viggers
Hair & Make-up Supervisor
   Deb Kenton
Assistant Supervisor **Jules Greenan**
Wigs Mistress **Jules Greenan**
Production Sound Engineer
   Ken Hampton
Number 1 Sound Operator
   Lucy Baker
Number 2 Sound Operator
   Javier Pando
Sound Engineer **Graeme Asher**
Sound Engineer **Richard George**
Sound Engineer **Greg Pink**
Radio Mic Assistant **Lisa Catton**
Communications and Marketing
   Stacey Healey
Communications and Marketing
   Sharon Atkinson
Digital Communications
   Tom Outing
Communications
   Leanne Woodhurst
Communications
   Emma Farley

Cast List

Phiip McGinley Jesus

Sophie Alvarez Bronfman Youth Chorus
Mary Andrews Chorus
Rachel Atkin Another Bad Soul / Devil
Gavin Baddeley Fourth Knight
Ruby Barker Mary
Christie Barnes Eve
David Barratt Centurion
Charlotte Barrs Youth Chorus
Faith Battersby Youth Chorus
Elly Beacon Youth Chorus
Becky Blackburn Angel / Chorus
Vikki Boddye Angel / Chorus
Janet Bowling Angel / Chorus
Paulina Bronfman Collovati Woman 2
Oliver Brooke Thomas / Judean Knight
Rosie Chivers Youth Chorus
Jean Christie Mother
Anne Collinson Chorus
Sue Collingwood Angel / Chorus
Mark Comer Joseph / Simon
Elizabeth Coombs Angel / Chorus
Diane Craven Courtier / Chorus
Maurice Crichton Herod / Devil
Ewan Croft Isaak / Youth Chorus
Robert Cummings King 1 / Roman Soldier
Frances Dalesman Angel / Chorus
Moira Davis Mary 2
Judy Diatta Angel / Chorus
Sarah Disney Courtier / Chorus
Aran Dolan John the Apostle / Shepherd
Alastair Dunn Doctor 1 / Chorus
Sheila Dunn Chorus
Catherine Edge Burgess 3
Wilma Edwards Elder
Elizabeth Elsworth Burgess 4
Anne Errington Attendant / Chorus
Mic Errington First Knight / Devil
Nigel Evans Lawyer 2 / Judean Knight

Jessica Farnhill Angel / Chorus
Roger Farrington Noah
Amelia Fordyce Youth Chorus
Claudia Freeman Youth Chorus
Felicia Freeman Youth Chorus
Paul French Caiaphas / Devil
Ian Giles Porter / Soldier 4 / Officer of the Watch 1
Toby Gordon Lucifer
Prue Griffiths Mary Sister of Lazarus / Courtier
Catherine Hall Anna
Roy Hargrave Poor Man
Guy Hawkyard Shepherd 1 / Roman Soldier
Hannah Hedley Brown Youth Chorus
Ottilie Hill Smith Daughter-in-Law 1 / Youth Chorus
Lilian Hogg Chorus
Tim Holman Peter
Joe Hopper Malchus
Linden Horwood Daughter-in-Law 3
Julie Howarth Pulleyn Chorus
Judith Ireland Burgess 1
Nita Jashari Angel / Youth Chorus
Andrew Jenkinson Doctor 2 / Chorus
Charlotte Johnson Youth Chorus
Harry Johnson Youth Chorus
Jim Johnson Beadle / Judean Knight
Anne Jones Angel / Chorus
Lorna Kennett Angel / Chorus
Mark Kennett Andrew / Officer
Martin Kirk Son 3 / Judean Knight / Matthew
Rebecca Lennon Youth Chorus
Imogen Ruby Little Mary Magdalene / Angel
Bob Mallow Adam / Second Knight
Lee Maloney Shepherd 2 / Roman Soldier
Philip Massey Pilate
Sam McAvoy Gabriel
Martina Meyer Attendant / Devil
Ehren Mierau Judas / Devil

Angie Millard Belzebub
Brenda Mitchell Angel / Chorus
Minori Mogam Youth Chorus
Rory Mulvihill Annas / Devil
Kathleen Murphy Courtier / Chorus
Ged Murray Lawyer 1 / Judean
    Knight
Amelia Neary Youth Chorus
David Newton Knight 2
Elizabeth Nolan Chorus
Simon O'Keefe King 2 / Soldier 1
Alastair Oliver Soldier 3 / Devil
Jennifer Page Woman
Bethan Parkinson Youth Chorus
Eva Parkyn Youth Chorus
Sue Pearson Chorus
Rachel Phillips Daughter-in-Law 2
Fiona Popplewell Youth Chorus
Freya Popplewell Youth Chorus
Dinos Psychogios Michael
Val Punt Women Caught In Adultery
Indie Star Ramsey-Wilson Youth
    Chorus
Barbara Revell Chorus
Harry Revell Nicodemus
Marcus Richardson Herod Antipas /
    Devil / Shepherd
Celia Roberts Youth Chorus
Sam Roberts Isaak / Youth Chorus
John Roden Abraham
Sandra Rowan Roman Magistrate /
    Angel / Chorus
Taylor Sanderson Messenger /
    Young James
Richard Sheils Lame Man / Judean
    Knight / Roman Soldier
Jill Shepherd Angel / Chorus
Bryan Shewry Third Knight / Thief on
    the right
Shiela Shouksmith Courtier / Chorus
Hannah Siddle Youth Chorus
Kate Siddle Angel / Chorus
Joan Sinanan Mary 3 / Courtier
Ian Small God
Loretta Smith Martha
Noël Stabler King 3 / Roman Soldier
Elizabeth Stanforth-Sharpe
    Precious Percula

Elizabeth-Mae Starbuck Angel /
    Youth Chorus
Di Starr Porter
Mick Taylor John the Baptist
Emily Thane Messenger / Another
    Good Soul
Simon Tompsett Joseph of
    Arimathea
Jennifer Tovey Youth Chorus
Paul Toy Bishop / Devil / Roman
    Magistrate
Liz Tune Angel / Chorus
Bernadette Turner Attendant /
    Servant / Chorus
Philip Turner Simon of Cyrene /
    Officer 2
James Tyler Thaddeus
Lisa Valentine Chorus
Samuel Valentine Simeon
João Rei Villar Zacchaeus / Shepherd
    / Thief on the Left
Neil Vincent Knight 1 / Devil / Older
    James
Nicola Waite Woman 1
Blair Wallace Blind Man
Mae Wallace Youth Chorus
Lucy Warren Youth Chorus
Michael Waters Lazarus
Gabriel Whalley Son 1 /
    Bartholomew
Patricia Williams Angel / Chorus
Shirley Williams Older Mary
Owen Williams Shepherd 3 / Phillip
James Wilson Son 2 / Soldier 2
Jennie Wogan Yet Another Bad
    Soul / Devil / Chorus
Cynthia Wood Burgess 2
Carla Woodcock Daughter in Law 1 /
    Youth Chorus
Yelyuzhou Xu Angel / Chorus

THE YORK MYSTERY PLAYS

in a new version by
Mike Poulton

For my godson,
Ben Hunt

List of Plays and Guilds Included

Numbers refer to the plays' positions in the original cycle.

4

Characters

GOD
GABRIEL
LUCIFER
MICHAEL
ADAM
EVE
NOAH
FIRST SON
SECOND SON
MOTHER
FIRST DAUGHTER-
   IN-LAW
THIRD SON
SECOND DAUGHTER-
   IN-LAW
THIRD DAUGHTER-
   IN-LAW
ABRAHAM
ISAAK
MARY
JOSEPH
FIRST SHEPHERD
SECOND SHEPHERD
THIRD SHEPHERD
FIRST KING
SECOND KING
THIRD KING
HEROD
MESSENGER
BISHOP
FIRST KNIGHT
SECOND KNIGHT
FIRST WOMAN
SECOND WOMAN

ANNA
SIMEON
JOHN THE BAPTIST
JESUS
FIRST OFFICER OF THE
   WATCH
SECOND OFFICER OF THE
   WATCH
FIRST LAWYER
SECOND LAWYER
WOMAN
FIRST ELDER
MARTHA
LAZARUS
PETER
PHILIP
PORTER
FIRST BURGESS
SECOND BURGESS
THIRD BURGESS
FOURTH BURGESS
BLIND MAN
POOR MAN
LAME MAN
ZACCHAEUS
PILATE
CAIAPHAS
ANNAS
FIRST DOCTOR
SECOND DOCTOR
JUDAS
SOLDIER
JAMES
MALCHUS

THIRD KNIGHT
FOURTH KNIGHT
SERVANT
DAME PERCULA
BEADLE
HEROD ANTIPAS
SIMON OF CYRENE
FIRST SOLDIER
SECOND SOLDIER
THIRD SOLDIER
FOURTH SOLDIER
THIEF ON LEFT
THIEF ON RIGHT
CENTURION
JOSEPH OF ARIMATHEA
LONGINUS
NICODEMUS
MARY TWO
MARY THREE
MARY MAGDALENE
THOMAS
BELZEBUB

And ANGELS, DEVILS, ARCHANGELS, KNIGHTS,
BISHOPS, COURTIERS, WOMEN, MEN, CHILDREN,
GUARDS, ATTENDANTS, DUKES, GOOD SOULS,
BAD SOULS, *etc*.

This text went to press before the end of rehearsals and so may differ slightly from the play as performed.

PART ONE

1. Barkers

GOD.

> Ego sum Alpha et Omega,
> Vita, Via, Veritas,
> Primus et Novissimus.

> I am gracious and great – God without beginning
> I am maker unmade – all might is within me –
> I am Life – and the way unto world's well-being
> I am foremost and first –
> As I bid it shall be.

> ANGELS *sing: 'Te Deum'*.

> Here, far beneath me, an isle shall I name
> Which isle shall be Earth! –
>   Into being I call
> Earth, here… And Hell… And this highest is Heaven –
> All truth in Creation shall dwell in this hall.

> GOD *creates Heaven, Earth, and Hell*.

> This I give you, mine angels,
> Whiles yet ye stay faithful…
> (*To* LUCIFER.) Nearest, and next in might after me,
> I make thee as master – my mirror in might –
> Blithest in bliss, my Arch-regent-to-be
> And name thee now – Lucifer! – Bringer of Light.

> ANGELS *sing: 'Sanctus, Sanctus, Dominus Deus Sabaoth'*.

GABRIEL.

> O merciful maker, full mickle thy might
> Who this work, with a word, hath right worthily wrought –
> Ever loved, love's creator, and maker of light
> All things out of darkness and chaos hast brought.

LUCIFER.

> What's that he says?
> *I* am glorious and great, and figured full fit –

The fairest of features on *my* face are fixed.
All wisdom I wield here, all worship, all wit –
In glory, in brightness, and blissfulness mixed.

MICHAEL.
Lord, with love lasting, we love thee alone –

LUCIFER.
Speak for yourself –

MICHAEL.
All-maker of might that hath framed us and marks us,
And wrought us right worthy to wait at thy throne
Where no failing, nor filth may befoul us nor soil us.

LUCIFER.
What! That's not right!
I'm most worthily made to be worshipped iwis
In glory I rise in my glittering gleams –
With fortitude framed my most might may not miss
I shall shine aye in bliss in my brightness of beams.
High in Heav'n I shall set me, full seemly to sight
Receiving due reverence through right of renown
I shall rise above Him that is highest on high
For I'm perfect, and noble –

LUCIFER *and his* ANGELS *are cast out of Heaven by*
ARCHANGELS *led by* MICHAEL.

                    O no! It's gone wrong!
Help, fellows! I'm falling! I'm going. I'm gone.

DEVILS (*left*).
We're thrown down from Heaven! Cast out – all forlorn!

DEVILS (*right*).
Lucifer – lurdan!

LUCIFER.
                    My wings are all torn!
Oh hell! What am I going to do now?
I'll go mad for woe! Now my wit is all went!

DEVILS (*left*).
Great gobfulls of filth – all our mirth shall be shent!
Out on thee, lumpkin, that lost us us light!

DEVILS (*right*).
> We shone once in bliss now we're blistered and brent!

LUCIFER.
> Oh hell and damnation – I've a mouthful of... Yeughhgh!

DEVILS (*left*).
> Out liar! Out sot! Tear him with our claws –

LUCIFER.
> Welaway! Woe! Now all's worse than it was.
> Why pick on me? – I never did nowt –

DEVILS (*right*).
> Oh yes you did – you brought us to nought!

DEVILS (*all*).
> To woe hast thou worked us –

LUCIFER.
> You lie! You lie, say I!

DEVILS (*all*).
> Thou 'rt the liar, Lucifer, and for it shalt thou pay.
> Here, lurdan! Have at you!

FIRST DEVIL.
> Let's scrag him, I say!

They beat up LUCIFER *and drag him off. Back in Heaven:*

2. Plasterers

GOD.
> In Heaven are angels fair and bright –
> Planets – stars wend their endless way
> The Moon I move to serve the night
> The Sun uprising lights the day.
>
> On Earth all trees and grasses spring
> Beasts and birds both great and small –
> Fishes in flood – all living things
> Thrive with my blessing, one and all.

Animals, birds, and fishes are created.

A thinking beast now will I make,
To keep this world and all therein,
In mine own likeness, mind, and shape,
So shall my love be seen in him.

3. Cardmakers

GOD.

Rise up, in blood and bone, thou clay
In shape of Man – I thee command.

ADAM *is created*.

A female from thy rib I'll make
Lest thou be lorn for lack of friend.

EVE *is created*.

Take from me now the breath of life...
And have ye both your souls of me.
This woman take thou to thy wife;
Adam and Eve your names shall be.

ADAM.

Ah, Lord full mickle is Thy might!
Thy love is seen on ilka side
O joyful is this blessed sight –
This wondrous world full broad and wide!

How many goodly things are here –
Of beasts and birds both wild and tame
Yet none in Thy likeness doth appear
Save we alone – Ah, loved be Thy name!

EVE.

To such a lord in high degree
Is due our love – love everlasting –
That raised us to such dignity
Placed above all other thing –

GOD.

Both wise and skilful shalt thou be –
You're made from clay but I made you well –
Lordship on Earth I'll grant to thee

In Paradise ye both shall dwell.
Love me, and love me aye therefore –
For making you, I ask no more.
Of good and evil you both shall learn
What to embrace and what avoid –

ADAM *and* EVE.

We shall be faithful evermore.

GOD.

Come – learn of me true lives to lead.

GOD *and his* ANGELS *lead them into Paradise.*

4. Fullers

GOD.

Adam and Eve here is the place
That I shall give you of my grace
To make your dwelling in.

Flowers, herbs, and fruit on tree,
Birds, and beasts – all that ye see –
Shall bow to you herein.

All for thy weal is here create –
All creatures bow in subject state –
Be fruitful – multiply!

They go to the Tree of Knowledge.

Save this tree alone,
Adam – I thee warn –
The fruit of it take none
For if ye take, ye die.

ADAM.

O Lord, that we should so do ill!
Thy bidding, sure, we shall fulfil
Faithful in thought, in word, and deed –

EVE (*butting in*).

Thy warning, Lord, we'll always heed.
This fruit untouched shall bide
Thou hast forbid...

5. Coopers

LUCIFER.

> Oh hell! My wits are baffled here,
> Moved in my mind with grievance great –
> That Godhead, which I saw so clear
> Knowing He would some wight create
> For majesty.
> Yet chosen from our angel-kind
> It should not be.
> Why not, since I was fair and bright? –
> And thought, therefore, I had the right
> To find most favour in His sight.
> Yet He distaineth me
> And chose His plaything – Man –
> To raise on high.
> And from that witless choice begins
> My bitter jealousy.
> But now He's made a mate for Man –
> In haste to her I will me hie,
> By guile to foil God's hateful plan
> Telling whatever lies I may –
> Eve! Eve!

EVE.

> Who's there?

LUCIFER.

> A fiend – a friend, I mean. It's only me.
> Of all the fruit that ye see hang
> In Paradise, why eat ye none?

EVE.

> Oh we may eat them every one
> Save this alone –

LUCIFER.

> And why the fruit of that same tree –
> More than another one?

EVE.

> The fruit thereof, nor Adam nor I
> May never go near –
> For we shall die,

God said, and end our solace here
In Paradise.

LUCIFER.
Ah, Eve! –
I know God well – it was His wit
So that from others should be hid
The virtues great that dwell in it.
Yet thou shalt see
Who eats the fruit of good and ill
Gains knowledge great as He.

EVE.
Say,
What kind of thing art thou
That tells this tale to me?

LUCIFER.
A worm –
And one that knoweth well
How ye shall worshipped be.

EVE.
What worship would we win thereby?

LUCIFER.
All lordship and all mastery. (*Gives her a mirror.*)
To greatest state ye shall be brought
If ye will do as I shall say.

EVE.
Never. No. We should be naught
Our God so ill thus to repay. No.

LUCIFER.
No?
As gods – His equal in everything?
Ay, gods ye both shall be!
Of good and ill to have knowing –
What's that but to be wise as He?

EVE.
Is this truth that ye say?

LUCIFER.
Yea – yea!

Believe in me –
Who never would, in any way,
Tell ought but truth to thee.

EVE, *after hesitating, takes a tiny bite – then greedy bites*.

Bite – bite on! – The taste is good.
Bear some to Adam – Amend his mood
And bring him too to bliss.

Exit LUCIFER. EVE *takes the apple to* ADAM.

ADAM.
Alas, woman – what is this?
For shame! Oh thou hast done amiss!

EVE.
Nay, Adam, grieve thee not a whit –
And shall I tell you the reason why?
A worm told me the truth of it
We shall be gods – both thou and I!
Bite – bite on! It is the truth
We shall be gods and know all thing –

ADAM.
To be called a god! Here, give me proof…
For once I'll follow thy leading.

He eats and then trembles with fear.

O Eve – in this thou art to blame
That to such sin enticeth me.
O look! I naked am!

EVE.
                    And so, I think, am I.

ADAM.
Alas! That this work we ever began!
This, this is evil, Eve, that thou hast wrought
And made this bad bargain –

EVE.
                    Nay, Adam! Blame me not!

ADAM.
Who then? Say, Eve – who then?

EVE.

> To blame the worm, more justice were.
> With tales untrue he me betrayed –

ADAM.

> Alas! Why ever gave I heed
> Or e'er believed thy lying words? –
> For here all woe's begun…
> Oh with what may my body be hid!

EVE.

> Let us take these fig leaves.
> What's done, is done.

ADAM.

> Forever I'd hide myself away
> From my Lord's sight if I once knew where…
> Oh how I fear!

GOD.

> Adam! Adam!

ADAM.

> Lord?

GOD.

> Where art thou? Where?

ADAM.

> I hear Thee, Lord, but see Thee not.

GOD.

> What reason, Adam, can there be?
> This wickedness – why hast thou wrought?

ADAM.

> The woman, Lord, misguided me
> And this disgrace on us hath brought.

GOD.

> Say, Eve, why did'st thou make this man
> To eat the fruit I bid should hang still?

EVE.

> It was the worm, Lord, tempted me
> Alas! – that I did a deed so ill!

GOD.

    Oh, wicked worm!
    For that thou in this manner
    Brought them to disobedience
    Have my malison forever!
    On thy belly thou shalt glide
    Forever full of enmity
    To all mankind on ilka side
    And filth it shall thy sustenance be –
    Thy meat and drink.
    Adam and Eve, also shall ye
    In earth forever sweat and swink,
    In sorrow, for your food.

ADAM.

    Alas! O let us rather sink –
    We that knew all the world's good!

GOD.

    Come, cherubim! Mine angels bright
    And drive these two to middle-earth.
    Banish them from my sight!

Enter ANGELS *led by* ARCHANGEL MICHAEL *with flaming sword.*

6. Armourers

MICHAEL.

    All creatures here to me attend.
    From God in Heaven am I sent
    Unto these wretches that wrong have bent
    Themselves so low.
    The joy of Heaven that them was lent
    Is lost them fro.
    Adam, take this. Here. (*Gives a spade*.) What do you think?
    In sorrow shall ye toil and swink
    To get withal thy meat and drink
    For evermore.
    And Eve, since thou beguiled him so,
    Travail hereafter shalt thou know –

Thy bairns thou shalt bear with mickle woe –
This I warn thee.

EVE.

Alas, for dole, what shall I do!
Now may I never rest nor rue.

ADAM.

And such a tale is told me too
Of swinking sore.
Now are we ruined, I and she too –
For evermore.

EVE.

What sorrow's here – what place is this?
I fear there'll be no end to woe.

ADAM.

Alas! How light is woman's wit
I well did know!

EVE.

If it be so it frets me sore.
But if that women witless are
Your mastery should have been the more
Against the guilt.

ADAM.

Nay! At my speech thou would never spare –
That hath us spilt.
For at my bidding you'd not let be
And all my woe I blame on thee –
Now, God let no man after me
Trust woman's tale till world shall end!

EVE.

Be still, Adam, name our guilt no more.
It may not mend.

They comfort each other.

ADAM.

He that us wrought, now guide us from woe
Where'er we wend.

MICHAEL *and the* ANGELS *drive* ADAM *and* EVE *out
of Paradise.*

7. Shipwrights

GOD.

> When first I wrought this world full wide,
> Wood and wind and waters wan,
> Heaven and Hell were seen by all
> Then, in my likeness, made I man –
> Lord and sire of middle-earth
> And woman gave I him to wive.
> I bade them wax and multiply
> True to my laws to lead their lives
> And people a world of harmony.

LUCIFER *leads* MEN *in a masque of sin.*

> But Man hath wrought so woefully –
> For sin holds sway and riots rife –
> That I repent me ruefully
> That ever I made or man or wife.
> This work I shall begin anew,
> Again this world shall be new-wrought
> And wasted all that dwell therein.
> Heaven's rain upon them shall be brought –
> Save Noah alone. Cease shall it not
> Till all be sunken for their sin.

> Noah, my servant, grave and pure.

GOD *appears to* NOAH, *who is very old and frail, being five hundred years old.*

> Noah, thy God – of great and small –
> Is come to warn thee of sorrows keen
> And marvels that shall after fall.
> Then, as I bid, do ye fulfil.
> I would, in haste, have wrought a Ship
> And though thou hast but little skill
> Fear not the work... for I shall help.

NOAH.

> Ah, worthy Lord, now take Thou heed!
> I am so old, and weak of heart
> That I can manage no day's deed
> Without great effort on my part.
> Though, Lord, Thy will be ever wrought –

As counsels each and ilka priest –
But ship-craft can I do right naught –
Ship-making know I not the least!

GOD.

Oh don't worry – it's easy.

NOAH *is not convinced.*

Choose three tall trees and hew them clean,
All by the square and nought a-squyn,
Saw them in boards, set battens between
Thus thrivingly, and none too thin.
Look that thy seams be subtly sewn
And nailed down so they will not part –
Thou, and thy sons, begin at once
Go call them forth and make a start

As NOAH *and his* SONS *begin to build the Ark,* NOAH
miraculously regains his youthful strength.

NOAH.

Ah, blissful Lord, that all doth hold,
I thank thee heartly both ever and aye
Five hundred winters I am old –
Methinks my years are as yesterday!
Right weak was I, and all unwield –
Now all my weariness is went away! (*Skips and dances.*)

GOD.

Noah, thy toil draws near its end,
Wrought right, as I instructed thee –

GOD *is about to touch the paintwork.*

NOAH.

Don't touch – the paint's not dry!

GOD.

Now listen carefully to me.
Of ilka beast thou shalt take two –
Both male and female – Is that clear? –
Into the Ark with thee they'll go –
All shall be safe you need not fear.
Thy wife, thy sons with thee also
And their three wives, to do them good.

Just these eight bodies, and no mo'
Shall thus escape the rising flood.

NOAH.

About this work now will I wend
With bird and beast my ship to fill.
He that to me this craft hath kenned
Doth guide us with His worthy will.

They load the animals.

9. Fishers and Mariners

NOAH.

My seemly sons and daughters dear
Attend ye now to what I say.

FIRST SON.

Father, we all stand ready here
Your bidding straightway to obey.

NOAH.

Go call your mother. And quickly, son.

SECOND SON.

What – Mother? You sure about this?

FIRST SON.

Fear not, Father. It shall be done. (*Exeunt* SONS.)

NOAH.

'All that lives under line
Shall someday pass to pine.'

FIRST SON.

Where are you, o Mother mine?
You must come to my father soon.

MOTHER.

Soon? Say'st thou so, son? Soon? Soon.

FIRST SON.

Aye, Mother.
My father thinks to flit full far

And bids you haste with all your main
To him, that nothing may you mar.

MOTHER.

Does he indeed? Flit back again
And tell him that I'm staying here.

FIRST SON.

Mother, I'd do your bidding fain,
But haste! Lest things go worse for thee.

MOTHER.

Go worse for me? That'll be the day! –
A day I would live long to see.

FIRST SON.

My father is ready to sail.
Mother, I warn you again.

MOTHER.

Come then – I shall not fail
To put a stop to his game.
Noah! Noah! Where art thou? Husband!

NOAH.

Lo, here at hand.
Come up here, wife! Quickly I pray!

MOTHER.

You're not getting me up in that thing!
What – climb up there you say?
You silly man, you're on your own!
Come, leave him, boys – I'm going home.

NOAH.

Nay? Good riddance then – have it your own way.
As usual! Who cares if you mun drown!

MOTHER.

Old fool, you'd best come down –
Find somewhat else to waste your time –
For shame!

NOAH.

Dame, forty days are nearly past
And gone since it began to rain,

Alive shall no man longer last
Save we alone – God's made that plain.

MOTHER.

Thou art stark mad, I am aghast,
Farewell! I'm going home again –

NOAH.

Oh woman, woman – art thou mad!
Of this my work thou knowest nowt –
All that hath or bone or blood
Must soon be overflowed wi't flood.

MOTHER.

Aye, sure! If you believe that –

The SONS *grab her*.

Wee! Ho! Out! Harrow!

NOAH.

Hold her, my boys, and bring her here –
Of her own harms she takes no heed –

SECOND SON.

Be merry, Mother, and mend your cheer.
The world will soon be drowned indeed!

She struggles.

MOTHER.

Alas, that I live these jests to bear!
Nay, nay – go home I must –
Don't you touch me – don't you dare!
I have a fowl to pluck, and truss!

NOAH.

Woman, woman, why doest thou thus?

MOTHER.

Noah, thou might have let me know!
Early and late you were always out
I sat at home, and off you'd go
Hither and thither and tells't me nowt.

NOAH.

It was God's will with never a doubt!

MOTHER.
Now by God's will thou'll get a clout! (*Attacks* NOAH.)

NOAH.
I pray thee, woman, be still!
Thus God would have it wrought.

MOTHER.
God should have asked me first,
If I'd agree to owt. (*Thunder: she is terrified.*)
Oooo! Help! Save me! Save me!

NOAH.
Now, wife, fear it never a deal
We shall be, sure, to safety brought.

MOTHER.
Then, should we 'scape from scathe
And so be saved, I think I ought
My gossips fetch – my cousins too
I wish they all were went in there.

She is about to fetch them.

NOAH.
To wade in the water some danger it were!
Look alive! Go up! No further ado.

MOTHER.
Alas! My life is full of woe
I've lived too long this burden to bear.

FIRST DAUGHTER-IN-LAW.
Dear Mother, never mind
For we shall wend with you.

They go in; the Ark sails.

MOTHER.
My friends all left behind
Are overflowed in't flood.

NOAH.
That we such grace should find
Now thank we all our God!

*A hymn of thanksgiving. Rain and storms. Sinners suffer.
Earth drowns. Ark sails.*

SECOND SON.

    Nine months are passed, 'tis plain,
    But the seas surround us still.

THIRD SON.

    God in His might and main
    May mend it when He will.

FIRST SON.

    Come, dear Father, look ye thereout –
    See if the water wane aught yet.

NOAH.

    (*Looking out*.) Before Thee, Lord, I sing and shout!
    The stormy clouds, I trow, are flit!

ALL SONS.

    Ah, Lord that bring'st all good about
    Eternal praise to Thee for it!

    NOAH *takes the Raven from its cage*.

NOAH.

    Of all the fowls that men may find
    The Raven is brave, and wise is he.
    Darkest winged of all thy kind
    Wend on thy way, I set thee free –
    Warily watch, and back return
    If thou dost find or land or tree.
    Nine months here have we been pined
    But when God wills, better may it be.

    Raven flies. They wait and perhaps sing.

FIRST SON.

    Father, this fowl is forth too long.
    Upon some land I trow he wends
    His food there for to find and fang –
    That makes him be a failing friend.

NOAH.

    Then another fowl full free
    Our messenger shall be.

    He takes the Dove.

    Over these waters wild and wide
    Fly, Dove, I pray thee – help us now –

Searching and seeking on ilka side
A sign that the floods are sunken low
That on the earth we might rest and bide
Bring us some token, that we may know
What tidings shall of us betide.

Dove flies.

SECOND DAUGHTER-IN-LAW.
Good Lord, look down on us
And cease our sorrows sere.

THIRD DAUGHTER-IN-LAW.
(*Bored.*) A twelve-month but twelve week
Have we bin swimming here.

Dove returns with an olive branch.

NOAH.
Now, boys, we mun be blithe and glad
And praise the name of Heaven's King
My bird hath done as I him bad
An olive branch I see him bring –
Come hither, my sons, in, hie!
All woe, away is went –
For certain there I spy and see
The hills of blessed Armenie.

MOTHER.
But, Noah, where now are all my kin
And company we knew before?

NOAH.
Drowned, Dame, drowned – Let be thy din!
(*Delighted by the thought.*)
Right sudden they bought their sins most sore.
And now good living let us begin
So that we grieve our God no more.

And, sons, He said – I wot well when –
'*Arcum ponam in nubibus*' –
Sets He His bow, for all to ken,
A token clear 'twixt Him and us –
A promise to all Christian men –
That though this world be ended thus
Ne'er shall it waste with flood again.

Rainbow appears.

Thus God of mickle might
Sets His sign full clear
High in the air –
The rainbow, there –
In all men's sight.

MOTHER.
Husband, since God, our Sovereign Lord,
Has set His sign thus certainly –
May we be sure that this same world
Shall last into eternity?

NOAH.
Nay, wife! That mun we not desire!
For, an we do, we toil in vain –
Next time it must be waste with fire
And never made a world again.

MOTHER.
With fire! Ah, Noah, you fright me sore
With these dread warnings ye say here!

NOAH.
Then be afraid, my wife, no more,
Certain, you've nowt to fear, my dear…
You'll be a long time dead by then –
Yea – by many a hundred year.

FIRST SON.
Father, how shall this life be led
Since none are in this world save we?

NOAH.
Sons, with your wives shall ye be stead
And multiply your seed shall ye.
All beasts and birds shall forth be bred
And our new world come into be.

They and the animals go into the new world.

10. Parchment-makers and Bookbinders

GABRIEL.

Abraham! Abraham!

ABRAHAM.

Lo, here I am.

GABRIEL.

Now tidings unto thee I bring
God will assay thy will and cheer,
If thou wilt bow to His bidding.
With Isaak, thy boy, thy son most dear
To the Land of Vision ye must repair
And there, of him, make offering.
I shall show ye right soon
The place of sacrifice –
God wills this deed be done
Obey, if ye be wise.

ABRAHAM.

Lord God that gave eternal light
This is a wonder strange to tell –
To take my son, seemly to sight,
Isaak the boy I love so well –
And unto death must he be dight?
Then sure God means this for our weal.

He stifles his grief and goes to ISAAK.

Isaak, my son, this news I bring
Into the wilderness must we wend,
And together there make offering,
Thus following our Lord's command.

ISAAK.

Father, I am at thy will alway
All God's commandments to obey.

ABRAHAM.

Come – let us be steadfast in His sight –

ISAAK.

And joyful return as go, I pray.
Young men bring forth our ass
With wood to fire our sacrifice.

YOUNG MEN *lead on an ass carrying a bundle of wood.*
They all begin the journey.

ABRAHAM.
My son, if God that reigns on high
Should of my life make His demand
I would be blithe for Him to die
For all our weal rests in His hand.

ISAAK.
Father, and even so would I –
Liefer than long to live on land.

ABRAHAM.
Ah, son thou sayest full sooth thereby
God give thee grace to steadfast stand.

You lads, bide ye here still
Further ye shall no mo'
For yonder I see the hill
Where Isaak and I must go.

ISAAK.
Keep well our ass and gear
Till we come again to you.

ABRAHAM.
My son, this load now must you bear
Till thou come high upon yon hill.

ISAAK *takes wood.*

ISAAK.
I take up my burden with right good cheer.
Who does God's bidding shall ne'er speed ill.

They climb the hill.

ABRAHAM.
Here,
Lay down your wood – yea – even here…
Here shall our altar builded be.

They build an altar.

ISAAK.
Father, we have both wood and fire
But nowt for our offering can I see.

ABRAHAM.

Trust, son, our Lord and sovereign sire
Who all provides in right degree.

They kneel and pray.

Great God that all this world hath wrought
And greatly governs good and ill
Grant me such strength that, as I ought,
Thy stern commands I may fulfil.
And if my flesh grieve or grudge Thee owt
Surely my soul assenteth still.
In burning all I have hither brought
Spare shall I not... whate'er I kill...
Dear son, I may no longer feign...
Thy sweet self is the bitter offering made.

ISAAK.

Why, Father... is it God's will I be slain?

ABRAHAM.

Yea, soothly, son – so hath He said.

ISAAK.

Then must I grudge Him not my pain.
To work His will shall I be glad.
Since thus He doth desire
I am prepared to be
Broken and brent in fire
Therefore, grieve not for me...

I think 'tis best that ye me bind
In bands full fast – both foot and hand –
Lest in the fear of death I mind
Your worthy purpose to withstand.
For you are old, and weak to wield
And I am young and wild of thought –

ABRAHAM.

To bind him that should be my shield!
Out on God's will! That I would not...
But lo, here must no force be felt
So shall God have what He hath sought. (*Binds* ISAAK.)

Farewell, my son, I must thee yield
To Him that this wide world hath wrought.

Now kiss me – from my heart I pray –
Take, Isaak, my last farewell for aye...

This is to me a peerless pain
To see my son thus laid on ground
I had far liefer I had been slain
Than see this sight – my child thus bound.

ISAAK.

Now farewell, middle-earth,
My flesh grows faint and cold
Now, Father, take thy knife
Do as our God ye told.

ABRAHAM.

Nay, nay, son – I beseech you yet –
Lie down, lie still now, hands and feet –
Thy words do make my cheeks to wet –

ISAAK.

Ah, dearest Father, life is sweet...
Yet do with me whate'er ye will
I ask no more respite.

ABRAHAM.

O Prince without Peer, I pray
Mine offering here to have it.
My sacrifice this day,
I pray Thee, Lord, receive it!

Raises the knife to strike.

GABRIEL.

Abraham! Abraham!
Good man, abide and stay thy hand –
Slay not the lad – do him nought amiss.
Lo, for your offering take this ram,
'Tis sent thee from the King of Bliss
That faithful aye ye both hath found.
Look that ye love Him, this He list
Loyal, and living after His law
For in your seed are all men blest
That shall be born both rich and poor.
If ye will still Him trow and trust
He shall be with you evermore.

12. Spicers

GABRIEL *holds a candida lily, and* ANGELS *sing first lines of an 'Ave Maria'*.

MARY.
What manner of greeting is this
That secretly comes to me?
For in my heart a thought there is –
What may betoken this vision I see?

GABRIEL.
Now dread thou nought, thou mild Mary,
Fear nothing that may ye befall
For thou hast found all sovereignly,
Of God, a grace above others all,
And in thy body's chastity
Conceive and bear a boy thou shall –
This salutation I bring to thee –
And Jesus the name ye shall him call.
Most mickle of might the child shall be
Lord over lords, and called God's son.
And David's seat, his father free,
Shall God give him – a kingly throne –
Reigning through all eternity.

MARY.
How may this be – conceive a child?
My maidenhood, in sooth to say,
I know no man hath e'er defiled –
In chastity have I lived aye.

GABRIEL.
The Holy Ghost on thee shall light
And over thee high virtue hold.
The blessed babe of thine born bright
Shall reign in Heaven and rule this world.

MARY.
Good angel, blessèd messenger,
God's will shall I fulfil alway
His handmaiden, lo! I am here
As thou hast said shall I obey.

ANGEL *departs leaving the lily,* MARY *sings 'Magnificat'*.

13. Pewterers and Founders

JOSEPH.

How long, o Lord, this life mun I lead?
My old bones weigh like lead
For I am of great eld,
Right weak, and all unwield.

Why do I thus beweep my fate?
I am beguiled – how, wot I nought –
My young wife is with child full great
And this me makes my cheeks to wet.
Certain, the child is none of mine
For me, she is a virgin clean –

He goes to MARY.

Gramercy, Mary, now what cheer...
Tell me in sooth how is't with thee?
Who has been here?
Thy womb waxeth great, I see.
Whose is it, Mary? Say.

MARY.

Sir, God's and yours –

JOSEPH.

Nay then, nay!

He turns away.

(*Aside*.) To me this is a careful case
Reckless I rave, reft is my peace
I dare look no man in the face –
Alas the day! Would I were dead!
Me loathes this life.
From Temple and all other stead
Every man's laughter will me drive –
Alas, why wrought thou so,
Mary, my wedded wife?

MARY.

For my witness great God I call
That in my mind ne'er wrought no miss.

JOSEPH.

Whose is the child thou art withal?

MARY.
> Yours, sir, and the King's of Bliss. (*Kneels and prays*.)
> Now great God of Your might
> That all may dress and dight
> Meekly to Thee I bow.
> Pity this troubled wight
> That into his heart may light
> The truth to believe and know.

JOSEPH.
> Who had thy maidenhead, Mary?
> Whose is the child?

MARY.
> Joseph, ye are beguiled
> With sin am I not defiled.
> God's hand is upon me seen.

JOSEPH.
> God's hand! Yah, Mary, God help us! (*Leaves her.*)

MARY.
> I pray to thee, King of Bliss
> Send him the truth of this
> In peace so may he bide.

JOSEPH.
> My heart's with great grief oppressed...
> Should I forsake her or nay?
> Now here for a time I must rest
> And sleep this long night away.

> *He sleeps.* GABRIEL *appears*.

GABRIEL.
> Joseph, awake! Take better keep
> Of Mary, thy helpmeet true and good.

JOSEPH.
> I'm full weary, sir – leave me to sleep –
> From walking and wandering in this dark wood.

GABRIEL.
> Nay – rise up and sleep no more,
> Thou makest her heart full sore
> That loves thee above all best.

JOSEPH.

>Say, what art thou?
>Or am I dreaming?

GABRIEL.

>Gabriel I am, God's messenger
>That hath taken Mary to my keeping.
>The boy that shall be born of her
>Is given of the Holy Ghost
>All joy and bliss shall be hereafter
>And to mankind of all the most.

JOSEPH.

>And is this sooth, Angel, thou says?

GABRIEL.

>In Bethlehem shall the boy be born
>Of God in Heaven the only son,
>Of man the most in might.

JOSEPH.

>Praise God! Now I was never so light! (*Goes home.*)
>Mary... Say, how doest thou –
>I would thou would me hear?
>My head, in shame, I bow...
>I ask forgiveness...

MARY.

>   Forgiveness, sir?
>Let be, for shame –
>For of such words ye have no need.

JOSEPH.

>Yea, Mary, yea, I am to blame
>For words too oft I to thee say'd.
>Now let us take up all our gear
>And such poor weeds as we shall wear
>And lay them in pack.
>To Bethlehem we must repair –
>I all alone this weight mun bear
>Help up now, on my back.

They set off for Bethlehem.

14. Tile Thatchers

JOSEPH.

> Alas! We've sought both up and down
> In Bethlehem each gate and lane
> So mickle folk are come to town
> For harbouring here we seek in vain
> In such a press.
> In sooth I can no succour see
> Save shelter with these gentle beasts.

They go into the stable.

MARY.

> God will us shield, full well know ye,
> Therefore, Joseph, be of good cheer
> For in this stable born will he be
> Shall save us from our sorrows sere.

JOSEPH.

> Then would I fain we had some light
> Whate'er befall –
> It waxes right murk unto my sight
> And cold withal.
> I will go find some light out there
> And wood to burn.
> Ah, Lord God, what weather is this!
> The fellest freeze that ever I feel'd.
> I pray God help the sick and eld
> And poor folk all that be unwield –

JOSEPH *goes.* JESUS *is born.* ANGELS *sing, off.*

MARY.

> Jesu! my son and saviour dear –
> Now is he born.
> Son, as I am simple subject thine
> Vouchsafe, sweet child, I pray thee
> I might hold thee in these arms of mine
> And in these poor weeds array thee.
> Grant me thy bliss.

JOSEPH.

> Ah, Lord God! What light is this

That comes shining thus suddenly? (*Goes in.*)
O, Mary, what sweet thing is that on thy knee?

MARY.

Jesus, my son, the sooth to say.

JOSEPH.

That I should live to see this day –
This mystery… (*Taking the child in his arms.*)
Now welcome, flower fairest of hue
I worship thee with main and might
Hail, my maker – Hail, Christ Jesu,
Hail, royal king, root of all right –
My saviour! My Lord! Sweet child!
Hail, blessed babe, bathed all in light
Hail, flower of the world.

MARY.

Oh, now sleeps my son. Blessed may he be –
And lies full warm these beasts between.

15. Chandlers

FIRST SHEPHERD.

Our forefathers what faithful were –
Hosea's one, and eke Isee –
Proved that a prince who peerless is
Should down descend to a laydee
And in Bethlem hard by
That same bairn should be born –

SECOND SHEPHERD.

And ere he be born in burgh hereby
Baa-lamb foretold, as I hear say,
A star shall shine forth and signify
Lightful of gleam like brightest day.

THIRD SHEPHERD.

Ah, merciful maker, mickle in might,
That thus will to Thy servants see!
Might we once get a look at that light
Gladder brethren might no men be.

ANGELS *appear.* THIRD SHEPHERD *is not looking*.

FIRST SHEPHERD.
Good heavens!

SECOND SHEPHERD.
                    Do you see what I see?

THIRD SHEPHERD.
What's up? What'st matter wi' ye?

THIRD SHEPHERD *sees* ANGELS, *and jumps*.

FIRST SHEPHERD.
Truly say –
Did y'ever see such a sight?

SECOND SHEPHERD.
No. Never. No… Not me.

THIRD SHEPHERD.
What a light! Ain't it bright!
As long as we have herdsmen been
And clapped us cattle in this clough
So strange a vision ne'er did us see.

FIRST SHEPHERD.
It must mean some marvel comin' to we.

An ANGEL *sings – tidings of* JESUS *born in Bethlehem.*

SECOND SHEPHERD.
What should it show? Who should he be?

THIRD SHEPHERD.
(*To the* ANGEL.) For all that ye can gurn and yawn
Us lads can sing as well as ye
Let's show 'em boys what we can do.
Right? Get ready… One, Two, Three:

The SHEPHERDS *sing their out of tune but spirited version
of the* ANGELS' *song.*

SECOND SHEPHERD.
Haha! This was a merry note –
And, by the death that I mun take
I have so croaked and dried mi throat
I need a drink, mi thirst to slake –

They all drink.

THIRD SHEPHERD.
　Ee that's better! Sup up!

They drink again.

FIRST SHEPHERD.
　The Angel brought us tidings new
　A babe in Bethlem should be born
　So spake the prophets sure and true
　And bade us greet him there this morn –
　This babe full mild.
　Now would I give both hat and horn
　To find that child.

THIRD SHEPHERD.
　To seek and search we'll have no need,
　And shall I tell the reason why? –
　That gurt bright star shall all us lead –

SHEPHERD TWO.
　Yea, sooth, thou say'st. Let's go thereby
　This babe to honour.
　And mak we mirth and melody
　To greet our saviour.

They go to Bethlehem, singing.

THIRD SHEPHERD.
　Yea, certainly this is the stead – (*Going in.*)
　Lo! Where the Lord is laid
　Betwixt two beasts his humble bed
　Right as the Angel said.

FIRST SHEPHERD.
　I kneel to thee, a simple man,
　Although I come of courteous kin,
　Lo, here, I bring you all I can –
　This broken brooch, and bell of tin
　At your bosom shall be.
　And when ye shall wield all the world
　Dear child, forget not me.

SECOND SHEPHERD.
　Too poor to give thee anything

As my heart would, and as I ought –
Two cob nuts here upon a string –
Look, little babe, for thee I've brought.

THIRD SHEPHERD.

Now look on me, my Lord, my dear,
Although I push me not in press,
Ye are a prince withouten peer,
I have no present you to please.
What's this? A horn spoon have I here
And it will hold 'bove forty peas –
This will I give with right good cheer
Such novelty may not displease.

ALL SHEPHERDS.

Farewell, thou sweetest swain
God grant us living long.
Now back to us flocks again
Mak merrie as we gang.

Exeunt singing. They are interrupted by the arrival of the
THREE KINGS *who enter separately, each with a rich train*
and music.

16 & 17. Masons and Goldsmiths

FIRST KING.

'Twas said a star with beams all bright
Over the East should glittering stand –
A star, a sign of mickle might
Of one who shall be Lord in land
And sinful men should save.

SECOND KING.

All wielding God, that all hath wrought,
I worship thee right worthily
That with thy bright star hath me brought
Far from my realm, rich Arabee.

THIRD KING.

God gave Mankind both Sun and Moon
And fixed yon star to stand stone still.

Till I its meaning light upon
God steer my steps with right good will.

The KINGS *see each other and greet each other with great
courtesy.* HEROD's MESSENGER *joins them. The* KINGS
continue their journey to Bethlehem together. MESSENGER
runs on ahead. Drums and trumpets. HEROD *in state – his*
KNIGHTS *and* BISHOPS *and* COURTIERS.

HEROD.
    The prince of all planets is outshone by me,
    The Moon at my bidding beams down on my grace,
    And Kaisers in castles fall down on their knees,
    For I'm witty and wise, and full fair of my face,
    Most glorious, victorious, and gayer than gold –

MESSENGER.
    (*Rushing in.*) Now then, Sir Herod – king wi't crown –

HEROD.
    Peace, clown! What the devil! – are ye so bold? –

MESSENGER.
    Oh sir! Great news is near this town!

HEROD.
    What, false losel? Does't me slight?
    (*To* SOLDIERS *who obey.*)
    Go bang yon boy and ding him down!

MESSENGER.
    My king, your messenger mun no man smite!
    These news may be for your renown –

HEROD.
    Get on wi' it then! He may be right.

MESSENGER.
    Great lord, I met this very morn
    Three kings what spoke together –
    Of a baby what's new born.
    And they're coming hither.

HEROD.
    Three kings you say? –

MESSENGER.

    They'll be here this day!

HEROD.

    Right then! Fetch us richest array.

    My men make merry – all joy and laughter –

    That no dissembling may be seen.

    (*Aside to* BISHOP.) Till we know what they're after.

    Enter KINGS.

    Now then, kings! 'Ow do?

FIRST KING.

    The Lord of everlasting light

    That brought us here from far-off lands,

    Keep thee, sir king, and these thy knights

    And all thy folk that here we find.

HEROD.

    Mahoun, my god, and most of might

    That gripes my kingdom in his grasp

    Now save you, sirs, seemly in sight –

    How can I do ye good? – Just ask.

SECOND KING.

    Good news we bring, great lord,

    A star stood us beforn

    Which makes us to enquire

    Of one that is new born.

HEROD.

    New born? So what? This news is daft –

    And sure, unwitty men were ye

    To flit so far to seek a lad –

    Who can this born babe be?

THIRD KING.

    O sir, he's come to be the king

    Of Jews and all Judee –

HEROD.

    He king! In't devil's name you lie!

    Now I see plain you rant and rave –

    I am't Jews' king, and none but I!

    Tek it from me, ye saucy knave,

That I am judge o'er all Jewry
To spill and spoil, or spare and save.

SECOND KING.

Lord, we ask nothing but your leave,
Over your lands to pass.

HEROD.

Pass whither, in't divil's name?
To seek a lad here in my lands?
False harlots, get ye gone – straight home –
Or ye'll be beat and bound in bands –

BISHOP (*aside*).

Great king, to foil this foul design
Let your right rage be set aside
And question them about this babe
So shall you quickly seek and spy
Their secrets and inten-ti-ons.

HEROD.

Yer right. Thanks for that – a timely interven-ti-on.
Now, kings! Let's cast all care away!
Since ye are friends and far from home
Look ye, my kingdom's laws obey,
On pain of losing life and limb.
And if that ye the truth will say
In peace both come, and go, ye may.
I might come with you, anyway.

FIRST KING.

Herod, we all accord
And say a babe is born
That shall be king and lord
And comfort men forlorn.

SECOND KING.

The trusty prophet true Ho-see
Full truly told in town and tower,
A maid of Israel – thus says he –
Shall bear one like the lily flower –

THIRD KING.

Foretold the child conceived shall be
Withouten seed of man's succour –

His mother a maiden pure and free
And he her son and our saviour –

HEROD (*aside to his* BISHOP).
Alas! The worse for me!
I am both down and done for!

BISHOP.
Courage, my king, be ye nothing abashed
This case to end shall well be brought.
Bid them go forth and friendly taste
The truth of this wonder they have sought
And tell it you… So may ye trust
Whether their tales be true or not.
Then may you kill them if ye list
And lay all waste that they have wrought.

HEROD.
Good man! Well said.
Any road up, you kings, I'm right, right glad.
Get you to Bethlem – 'tis near at hand –
Enquire you there for this newborn lad
Of him that should be lord in't land.
Then come back here to me you shall
To tell the truth of what ye find.
To worship him too – that's my will –
Such devotions surely ye'll understand?

SECOND KING.
Certes, great king, we'll come again
To tell you of this wondrous child.

HEROD.
And see yer do, as ye be men.

Exeunt KINGS.

BISHOP.
Farewell, you fools – ye are beguiled!

HEROD.
Now shall they surely take their trace
And tell me of that swittering swain
And all their counsel in this case.
If it be true they'll all be slain
No gold shall buy them better grace!

Exeunt HEROD *and* COURT. *The* THREE KINGS *journey to Bethlehem.*

FIRST KING.

Hail, fairest of fair, all folk for to find,
From the Fiend and his fellows us faithfully fend.
(*Gives gold.*)

SECOND KING.

Hail greatest and best, born here to unbind
All souls fallen prey to the wiles of the fiend.
(*Gives frankincense.*)

THIRD KING.

Hail, flower, the fairest that never shall fade,
Hail, son sent to shield us from sins our sires made.
(*Gives myrrh.*)

ALL KINGS

Hail, man, that is born here all mankind to save
Hail, prince in thy triumphing over the grave.
Our faith here confessing – good babe –
Give us thy blessing.

They kneel in adoration, then come out.

FIRST KING.

Now let's return to Herod the king
Remembering the promise we made

SECOND KING.

He'll come here himself with offering
For this sweet child –

THIRD KING.

Or so he said…

What's this I see?

They set off for Bethlehem. GABRIEL *appears.*

GABRIEL.

Turn courteous kings – give heed to me.
From God himself I here am sent
To warn you as a faithful friend –
Herod the king hath mischief meant
And plots with shame your lives to end.

Lest ye take harm by his intent
By other ways God wills ye wend. (*Exit* GABRIEL)

THIRD KING.
You heard what the young man spake to me?

SECOND KING.
Sirs, hurriedly I say we flee –

THIRD KING.
Each to his own lands secretly –

FIRST *and* THIRD KINGS.
And we agree.

Exeunt the THREE KINGS *in different directions.*

18. Marshalls

GABRIEL.
I Gabriel, God's angel bright,
Bid thee, Joseph, flee this night.
Herod the king will strike stark dead
All boy children in each homestead –
Then, while he lives – Away!
Till I shall fetch ye home again
In Egypt shalt thou stay.

JOSEPH.
Alas, what ails this king to spill
The blood of babes that ne'er did ill?
Mary, my darling dear –

MARY.
Say, Joseph, love, what cheer?

JOSEPH.
Out of our kith where we are known
Right quickly mun we be withdrawn
Both thou and I.

MARY.
Dear Joseph, why? Conceal it not –
To sorrow, say who hath us deemed?

What are the harms that we have wrought
Wherefore we must be blamed?

JOSEPH.

Wrought we harm? Nay, nay, you're wrong
And wit thou well it is not so.
Our young lad's life we must forgo
Unless we flee fast from his foe.

MARY.

His foe? Alas! Now by my faith
Who would my sweet babe do to death?
I tremble for fear.
When may my share
Of evils end?

JOSEPH.

I warn thee he is furious threat
With Herod, king, hard harms to have.
With thy sweet son – if he be met –
There is no salve that may him save.
I pray thee, Mary, wrap him warm
For we must wend right many a mile
And when thou needs must ease thine arm
Shall give me him to bear a while.
In all our need
God will us speed;
This sure I say.

MARY.

God keep us all
As best He may.

19. Girdlers and Nailers

MESSENGER.
  Mahoun withouten peer
  King Herod save and see!

HEROD.
  Now then, mi lad, come here –
  Say how are things with thee?
  What tidings have ye? Any?

MESSENGER.
  Yea, king. Since I last was here
  I've been gallopin' everywhere
  And marvels I've seen full many.

HEROD.
  Oh aye?

MESSENGER.
  I met two towns between
  Them kings with gold crowns a-gleam
  Riding right royally.

HEROD.
  Oho! By sun and moon
  Will I get them in my sight!
  All three will be here soon –
  We'll hear their tales tonight.

MESSENGER.
  Nay, king, that game is done.

HEROD.
  Eh? What are yer trying to say?

MESSENGER.
  I think they've run away

HEROD.
  You're having me on. You jest!

MESSENGER.
  I swear, king, they've gone past.

HEROD.
  'Scaped clean away from me?

MESSENGER.
    As fast as fast may be.
    Gone home – all three – they've fleed.

HEROD.
    Ah, dogs! The devil ye speed!

MESSENGER.
    They made their offering
    Unto the child new born
    They swear he shall be king
    And wear a kingly crown –

HEROD.
    Alas! Then I'm undone!
    Fie on them traitors – Fie!
    Will they beguile me thus?

MESSENGER.
    All heard them prophesy
    And name his name 'Je-sus'.

HEROD.
    Fie, naughty lad! You lie!

HEROD *swoons into the arms of his* BISHOP.

BISHOP.
    Hence, dog! Unless ye fly
    That frights him in this wise.
    In chains thou here shalt die!
    Thou liest, false traitor strong!

MESSENGER.
    'Ere – keep yer miter on!
    You'll bust a gut, Yer Grace.

BISHOP.
    Dar'st look me in the face!

HEROD.
    Upon my life and limb
    I will that baby bang!
    On high I will him hang
    Both thee, my lad, and him!

MESSENGER.

> Why should I take the blame?
> Now farewell, all the heap.

BISHOP.

> Go, in the devil's name –
> Or I shall make thee skip!

HEROD.

> What the devil am I going to do?

BISHOP.

> Great king, amend your cheer
> Let nowt your mind annoy
> My counsel you shall hear
> This babe we must destroy.
> Then summon up your knights
> And bid them ding to death
> All baby boys they find
> In Bethlehem alive.

HEROD.

> Oh excellent! Very good, bishop!

BISHOP.

> We will wend with you then
> To ding that dastard down.

HEROD.

> *Aux armes*, then, each and ilka man
> That holds faith in Mahoun!

Exeunt HEROD *and* COURT.

FIRST KNIGHT.

> Come, fellows all, come here.
> Ye know what must be done.
> What bastards have we there?

FIRST WOMAN.

> Out on you! Thieves, I cry!
> What, would you slay my son?

SECOND KNIGHT.

> These brats shall dearly buy
> This bale that we've begun.
> Let go, therefore, and fast.

FIRST KNIGHT, *seizing a child from its mother*.

SECOND WOMAN.
Oh lest for dole, I die
To save my son shall I
Aye while my life shall last!

She beats FIRST KNIGHT.

FIRST KNIGHT.
Cursed dame! The devil thee speed –
Me too, but that blow be quit!

FIRST WOMAN.
To die I do not dread –
I warn thee well to wit –
To save my boy, my dear.

They attack KNIGHTS, *throwing mud and beating them with pots, pans, brooms, etc*.

FIRST KNIGHT.
Aux armes! for now is need.
Unless we do this deed
These queans will quell us here.

KNIGHTS *kill all the babies*.

SECOND WOMAN.
Alas! This wicked strife
No bliss more may I get –
This knight upon his knife
Hath slain my son so sweet.

WOMEN *pelt* KNIGHTS *with mud, and give them a good beating*.

FIRST KNIGHT.
The devil now speed you both!
Away! Why rave ye so!

SECOND KNIGHT.
Ye shall not 'scape from scathe –
This sword shall make ye go.

FIRST WOMAN.
False knights, I say you lie!

SECOND KNIGHT
>Let's turn us backs and fly.

KNIGHTS.
>Run away! Run away!

>KNIGHTS *are chased out*.

FIRST WOMAN.
>Alas, that we were wrought
>In world, women to be.
>Our babies killed!

SECOND WOMAN.
>These babes so dear we bought
>Here, in our sight to see
>Dispiteously spilled.

>*Exeunt. Enter* HEROD *and* COURT.

FIRST KNIGHT.
>Mahoun our god of might
>Now save thee, Herod king!

BISHOP.
>Sire, welcome home your knight
>He'll tell you great tiding
>Of jests where they have been.

HEROD.
>But did it go all right?
>Speak now – hast done this thing?
>Tell all that ye have seen.

SECOND KNIGHT.
>Sire, as ye bade us, we have done.

HEROD.
>Then, sirs, I swear by Moon and Sun
>Ye are right welcome – welcome home!
>But are ye sure you've gotten this groom?

FIRST KNIGHT.
>None of them, sire, escaped your doom
>All baby boys are dead and gone.

SECOND KNIGHT.
> We witness well that there are none
> Alive in Bethlem town.

HEROD.
> Had ye slain a thousand score
> I would rejoice and laugh the more!
> Now all my fears are fled
> I shall sleep sound in mi bed.
> Come, now, come to your reward!

> *Exeunt omnes rejoicing.*

41. Hatmakers, Masons, and Labourers

ANNA.
> I tell you all, here in this place
> By God's virtue in prophecy
> That one is born to our solace
> Here to be present certainly,
> Within short space.
> A widow I these threescore year –
> And four years too – the truth to tell:
> Here have I tarried with good cheer
> For the redemption of Israel.

SIMEON.
> Ah, blessed God, be thou my shield
> And solace me both night and day;
> In heaviness my heart I yield,
> Unto myself, lo, thus I say,
> For I am weak and all unwield.
> Out of this world I would away
> Thus wax I worse, and worse alway.
> Now sure then should my joy begin
> If I might see him – of him tell –
> The one who's born withouten sin
> And for mankind makes mirth to dwell –
> Ah, well were me for ever and aye
> If I might see that babe most bright,
> Ere I were buried close in clay.

GABRIEL.

> Friend Simeon, God's servant right
> Bold words to thee I bring, this day.
> The Holy Ghost, made most in might,
> Decrees thou shalt not die away
> Till thou hast seen
> Jesus, the babe that Mary bore,
> For all mankind to slake their care
> And comfort bring to less and more
> Both morn and e'en.

SIMEON.

> Ah, Lord, Gramercy now I say
> That thou this grace has to me plight,
> Ere I be covered here in clay
> To see that glorious beam burn bright
> Jesus my joy, my saviour aye;
> Blest be his name!

MARY.

> Full forty days are came, and went,
> Since Jesus, my sweet babe I bore
> Therefore I must him here present –
> Here in the Temple after God's law.

JOSEPH.

> Therefore now dress we forth our way.
> We must, withouten any doubt,
> An offering make to God this day,
> With hearts devout.

MARY.

> But we should offer beast and fowl –
> Two dove birds and a lamb also –

JOSEPH.

> Well, Mary, we have dove birds two
> And if we have no more to bear –
> A lamb with them, as rich men have –
> I think that we must offer here
> Jesus our babe as we vouchsafe
> Before God's sight.

MARY.

> Unto my God, highest in Heaven

And to the priest ordained by skill
Jesu, my babe, I offer him,
Here with my heart and right goodwill.

SIMEON.

Ah blessed babe, welcome thou be.
Born of a maiden in chastity.

ANNA.

Welcome, thou our succour
Welcome with all honour
Here to this Minster.

SIMEON.

Hail, royal rose, right ruddy of hue
Hail, flower unfading, both fresh aye, and new,
Hail, kindest comfort that man ever knew,
Our greatest truth.

I thank thee, Lord God, of thy great grace
That thus has spared me for a space
This babe in mine arms to embrace
By prophecy told.

He holds the child.

Now come to me Lord of every Land
Come mighty king of seas and strand
Come bringer of joy to tower and town
Come my Redeemer I am thine own!

JOSEPH.

Mary, my spouse and maiden mild,
In heart I marvel wonderfully
How these folks speak thus of the child
And tell of the world's mastery.

MARY.

Yea, sure, Joseph, I marvel also
But I shall treasure it in my heart.

JOSEPH.

God give him grace great good to do,
And thou and I shall play our part.

SIMEON.

Hark, Mary I shall tell thee truth ere I go

This child was sent here to win us from woe
In redemption of many and recovery also
Mark what I say.

And the sword of sorrow shall thy heart thrill
When soothly thou shalt see him suffer ill
For the weal of all wretches, as is God's will
Upon a day.

Farewell, the royalest rose that is reigning
Farewell, the babe best in thy bearing
Farewell, God's son. Grant us thy blessing
Always.

Transitional music – we move on to JESUS *in his manhood.*

21. Barbers

JOHN THE BAPTIST.
　　Almighty God, Lord verily
　　How wonderful is man's lying!
　　For though I teach them, day by day,
　　And tell them, Lord, of thy coming
　　That all hast wrought
　　Men are so dull that my preaching
　　Goes all for nought.

　　When, Lord, I have in name of thee
　　Baptised the folk in water clear –
　　Then have I said that after me
　　Shall come another – greater in power
　　Than I at best.
　　He shall baptise them more entire
　　With fire
　　And the Holy Ghost.

GABRIEL.
　　O, John, take heed what I shall say
　　I bring thee tidings wondrous good
　　Jesus, my Lord, shall come this day
　　From Galilee unto this flood

Ye Jordan call.
And baptism shall take, in mildest mood,
This day he shall.

JOHN.

But well I wot Baptism is ta'en
To wash and cleanse a man of sin
And well I know that sin is not
In him – without him or within.
What needs he then
To be thus cleansed of any sin
Like wicked men?

JESUS.

O John, ye know mankind is weak,
And to mankind I have me knit –
Then, since I am made man in kind,
That men should me their mirror make
I have their frailty in mind,
So thus do I this baptism take.
For man's sake.
Full openly.

JOHN.

Most mighty Lord, great is thy grace
Great as the work thou dost prepare.

JESUS.

Come, John, baptise me in this place.

JOHN.

Forgive me, Lord. I do not dare
To let this be.
For, Lord, methinks there is more need
Thou baptise me.

JESUS.

Thou say'st full well, John, certainly.
But suffer now, for heavenly need
That righteousness be by thine aid
Fulfilled in word, and thought and deed,
Through baptism clear.
Come, baptise me in my manhood
Openly here.

JOHN.

    Then help me, Lord, through thy Godhead –
    Draw near…
    Jesu, my Lord whose love is most
    Here I baptise thee in the name
    Of Father, Son, and Holy Ghost.
    But in this deed, Lord, set no blame
    This day on me
    And bring all souls to Paradise
    That trust in thee.

    Dove descends. ANGELS *sing 'Veni Creator'.*

22. Locksmiths

LUCIFER.

    Get outta my way! (*Shoving through the crowd.*)
    Forgotten me?
    What makes here all this crowd and throng?
    Get ye all hence! Move! I cannot see –
    I must have been away too long…

    Since the beginning, when I fell
    For my high pride, from Heaven to Hell
    On Earth I go about to tell
    To all mankind
    How I in fires shall make them dwell
    Forever pined.

    And now some men speak of a swain
    How he shall come and suffer pain
    And by his death to bliss again
    Shall they be brought.
    But sure they tell their tales in vain –
    I count it nought.

    For everything I know, I ween,
    Of that young swain those men must mean
    How he has in great anguish been
    Since he was born –
    And suffered mickle sorrows keen
    Evening and morn.

And now by chance it so falls out
This lozel that they're on about
To Wilderness is he went out
All on his own.
And who shall crush him? Have no doubt –
I am the one.

He's fasted long – that mars his mood –
These forty days withouten food
If he be born of flesh and blood
He hungers ill.
With gluttony I deem it good
To try his will.

(*To* JESUS.) Thou witty man and wise of rede
If thou knowst aught of thy Godhead
Bid now these stoned be turned to bread
Before us two –
Thus may they stand thyself in stead
And others too.

JESUS.
O wretched wight – thy wits are wood –
'Twas writ for all who understood
A man lives not in might and mood
By bread alone –
But God's own words are ghostly food
To men each one.

LUCIFER.
Such carping cant I never heard.
He's not as hungry as I feared.
Then since his Father helps him here
By subtle sleight
Let's see if he dare climb up there –
This Minster's height.

(*To* JESUS.) I say.
If thou be God's son, full of grace,
Let's see your courage in this place
To prove thy might.
Get up there – then fall down on thy face
Here in my sight.

For it is writ, as well is kenned,
How God to thee shall angels send
And they shall hold thee in their hend,
Where'er thou go
That thou shalt on no stone descend
To hurt thy toe.

JESUS.

Warlock, let be, thy lies are vain –
Is it not writ – I say again –
Thy God thou shalt not tempt, or pain,
With thy discord?
Nor quarrel shalt thou none maintain
Against thy Lord.

LUCIFER.

Eh up. Mi labour is in vain –
Defeat I can't abide.
He proves he is a mickle prize
Therefore it's good I me advise
And since I may not in this wise
Make him my thrall.
I'll try this time with covertise
To make him fall.

(*To* JESUS.) I hope ye know, since it is so,
That I'm the sovereign of us two,
Yet to reward thee ere I go
I shall not fail.
This – if thou wilt assent thereto –
Ye shall do well.
For mine is all this world to wield
In tower and town, forest and field
And if thy soul to me ye'll yield
And humbly bend,
Then I shall be thy sword and shield
And faithful friend.
Look out there, sir – where thou may see
Many a kingdom and country –
And all this shall I give to thee
For evermore,
If thou will bend and kneel to me...
All this I swear.

JESUS.

> Cease from thy swaggering, Satan! Ass!
> I grant thee no thing thou doest ask.
> For it is writ, for all to read,
> The Lord God shalt thou hold in dread
> And honour aye –
> Serving Him in word and deed
> Both night and day.
> Hence! I command thee – Back to Hell
> And keep thee there
> In fellowship with foul fiends fell
> For evermore.

MICHAEL *and* ANGELS *enter.*

LUCIFER.

> Eh up! I dare not look, alas!
> Now all is worse than ever it was
> He musters all the might he has –
> High let him hang!
> Follow who will, for I must pass
> To torments strong.

MICHAEL, GABRIEL *and armed* ANGELS *drive*
LUCIFER *away.*

MICHAEL.

> Methinks that ye were foul misled,
> Lord, by this fiend that is now fled.

JESUS.

> Mine Angel dear, be not afraid
> The Holy Ghost my way hath led
> And does so still.
> For when the fiend mankind shall see
> Assailing them in dire degree
> They may a mirror make of me
> And fear no ill.
> Then overcome they shall not be...
> Unless they will.

24. Capmakers

FIRST OFFICER OF THE WATCH.
> Look lively lads – don't gape and stand!
> Right smartly now get ready your gear,
> This filly we in folly found
> Let's show her what she has to fear.

SECOND OFFICER OF THE WATCH.
> I'll bear witness, by my hand,
> How we surprised her unarrayed
> Against the laws of this our land –
> All naked with her lover laid.

FIRST OFFICER OF THE WATCH.
> What's more he was a wedded man
> And hers is such a wicked sin –

FIRST LAWYER.
> Her mischief shall she bitter ban
> And smart when we our case begin.

SECOND LAWYER.
> Ah, false stud-mare and stinking whore!
> How durst thou sneak and steal away
> To sore offend against our law
> And do thy vile adultery?

SECOND OFFICER OF THE WATCH.
> Her harlotry she'll sorely buy
> For what we saw, we shall report.

FIRST LAWYER.
> She shall be stoned to death today,
> Come drag the slut before our court.

FIRST ELDER.
> Be not so fierce, good sirs – abide!
> If you will hearken unto me –
> That prophet from the countryside
> E'en now draws near our courts, I see.

SECOND LAWYER.
> Master, draw near, we bid you say
> What judgment pass we in her case?
> Shall we our ancient laws obey
> Or shall we their just force efface?

JESUS *writes in the sand with his finger for a while before answering.*

JESUS.

Right well I see your hidden thoughts
And what meaning ye have in mind.
Ye lawyers, long that law have taught,
Be not to its true meaning blind.

My judgment now hear ye
I say these words alone –
Let he that from all sin is free
Cast the first stone.

SECOND LAWYER.

I'm put in mind of mine own sin.
I'll leave you here. For I have done.

FIRST LAWYER.

Thus do our troubles all begin
So much for law! I'd best be gone.

SECOND OFFICER OF THE WATCH.

And since the law has fled the field
Its officer shall straight go home.

JESUS.

Woman, say now where those men went
That keenly have accusèd thee?
To stone thee here was their intent.

WOMAN.

Lord, no man has condemnèd me.

JESUS.

Neither do I condemn. Repent.
As from thy fault I make thee free,
Look ye no more to sin assent.

WOMAN.

Ah, Lord! Forever love be thine.
All earthly folk me hear
Honour him and his high name
That me from stain doth clear
And saves from sin and shame.

MESSENGER.

Jesu, thou prophet, I come to say

My ladies Martha and Marie
If you vouchsafe, they would thee pray,
To come in haste to Bethany.
Lazarus whom thou lovedst alway
Is sick, and like, Lord, soon to die.

JESUS.

Nay Lazarus is dead today.

They all go to Bethany, to the tomb of LAZARUS.

MARTHA.

Alas for ruth now may I rave
And feebly fare by wood and field,
Would God that I were in my grave –
That death might take me from the world.

MARY.

Of Jesus I will comfort seek
For he shall be my strength and shield.

JESUS.

(*Kneels to pray.*) Father, vouchsafe of thy great might
That all these folk, both young and eld,
Who stand and bide to see this sight
May truly trow that to this world
Where here this time I pass,
'Tis Thou hast me sent.
Lazare, Lazare, *veni foras*!
Come forth from thy monument!

Stone rolls away, LAZARUS *comes out of the tomb.*

LAZARUS.

Ah, peerless prince, of pity free,
Worshipped be thou in world alway
That thus hath shown thy might in me,
Both dead and buried many a day.
By certain signs here men may see
Thou art God's son, and verily.
And all who truly trust in thee
Shall never die!

MARY.

Here men may find a faithful friend
That thus recovers us from care.

MARTHA.
>Jesu, my Lord and master kind
>For this we bless thee evermore.

JESUS.
>Sisters, I make no longer stay,
>To other folk now must I fare,
>Toward Jerusalem lies my way
>For works must be accomplished there.

25. Skinners

Enter PETER *and* PHILIP *with a donkey, chased by*
a PORTER.

PORTER.
>Stay! What are ye that steals away
>My donkey here – ye brazen knave!

PETER.
>Sir, by your leave, we kindly pray
>This beast to have.

PORTER.
>Oh? To what intent ye first shall say
>Or else ye'll none.

PHILIP.
>Our master, sir, that all may save,
>Asks for this one.

PORTER.
>And what man's he ye master call?

PETER.
>Jesus of Nazareth, Lord of us all,
>Hath need of him.

PORTER.
>Sirs, take the beast and forth now fare
>Ye're welcome to him.

He goes to the city.

Oh, sirs, I have good news to tell
And trust it fully – all is true –
Here comes a son of Israel,
I mean the prophet called Jesu
Lo, this same day
Hither in state. These tidings new
Believe ye may.

FIRST BURGESS.

And is that prophet, Jesus near?
Of him I've heard great wonders told –
He does great marvels far and near
He heals the sick both young and old
And to the blind gives sight –
Both deaf and dumb – whoe'er he would –
He cures outright.

SECOND BURGESS.

With loaves but five, five thousand men
He fed, and each one had enow.
Water he turned to wine, and then
He made corn grow withouten plough
Where ere was none.
Dead men he brought to life again –
Lazar was one.

THIRD BURGESS.

Oft in our Temple would he preach
Against false folk that loved abuse
And also new laws would he teach
Against the old law long in use
And – thus sayeth he –
'Bad laws must all give way to truth!'
Well, we shall see…

FOURTH BURGESS.

Methinks, good sirs, ye judge right well
And good reports of him ye bring
And since we all this matter feel
Go we to greet him as our king
And Christ him call.

PORTER.

Of all the Jews I'll hail him king.

OMNES.
> So shall we all!

They approach the city singing and rejoicing.

BLIND MAN.
> Ah Lord that man on mould hath made,
> Both Sun and Moon, and night and day,
> What noise is this that makes all glad
> From whence it wends I cannot say.

POOR MAN.
> Why, man, what ails thee thus to cry?
> Where would thou be? Lo, I am here.

BLIND MAN.
> Ah, sir, a poor blind man am I
> And aye have been from tender year –
> I pray you tell what it may mean –
> This mirth I hear both loud and clear –
> What have you seen?

POOR MAN.
> Jesus, the prophet draweth near
> And this I ween
> Is the rejoicing that ye hear.
> Through all this town.

BLIND MAN.
> Sir, help me to the street, I pray
> That I might hear…
> Jesu, thou son of David bold,
> (*Calling above the noise.*) Pity my plight!
> Alas! I cry – he hears me not –
> He has no pity for my care.
> He shuts his ear – what cares he aught?

POOR MAN.
> Cry louder, man – and do not spare,
> Beg for thy sight.

BLIND MAN.
> Jesu, thou healer, art thou there?
> Pity my plight!

PETER.
> Lord, grant his boon, and his asking

And let him wend.
We'll get no peace until this thing
Be brought to end.

JESUS.

What would'st thou, man? What dost thou ask?
Beforn us all, say openly.

BLIND MAN.

Lord, thy light to me is lost.
Now grant it me – I cry mercy –
This would I have.

JESUS.

Blithely with cheer lift up those eyes
Thy faith hath saved.

BLIND MAN.

Thou King of Bliss, loved may ye be
That thus my sight hath sent right soon.
I that was as blind as any stone
By thy great skill,
Now see right well!

LAME MAN.

For mercy, cast your mind on me
And help me, Lord, as well ye may.

JESUS.

Now cast those crutches far from ye
Here in this field.
And as in truth ye steadfast be
Ye are healed.

LAME MAN.

Lord, lo, my crutches where they fly
As far as I away may fling
I am as blithe as bird in sky
Ere that was halt and lame of limb.
Be loved alway!

ZACCHAEUS.

Here stand I, troubled much in mind,
Since chief of tax gatherers am I,
Sight of this Lord I cannot find
For though I would have come him nigh

And would him meet –
You see I'm small
And men right tall
Throng all the street.
Then to that sycamore I'll go
And climb up high
Then under me
The Lord I'll see
If he pass by. (*Climbs the tree*.)
Until the prophet come this way
Here shall I bide whate'er befall.

JESUS.

Zaccheus, from that branch come down.

ZACCHAEUS.

Lord, at thy word, in haste, I shall...
And tarry not. (*Comes down fast*.)
'Fore thee, upon my knees, I fall,
For sins I've wrought.
My sins me shame – but I'll repent –
Forsake past sin, and henceforth will
Give all my wealth that is unspent
Unto poor folk, to stay them still –
This will I fain.
Those I beguiled, to them I will
Restore again.

JESUS.

So may thou hope for lasting life.
Farewell, Zachee.
Disciples dear give heed to me.
Unto Jerusalem shall we ascend
Where Son of Man betrayed shall be
And given into his enemies' hend
With great despite –
Spitting and shame on him to spend
And sore to smite.

I mourn, I sigh, I weep o'er you
Jerusalem, on thee to look,
And weep ye too
That ever you your king forsook
To me untrue.

For stone on stone shall none be left
Down on the ground shall all be cast –
Thy game, thy glee, all from thee reft,
To pay thy sin, and evils past.
To me unkind –
Against thy king hast thou trespassed
Keep this in mind.

*The donkey is brought. Palm Sunday Anthem. Procession
into Jerusalem on donkey.*

MEN *and* WOMEN.
Hail, prophet proved, withouten peer!
Hail, Prince of Peace, that shall endure!
Hail, comely king, courteous and clear!
Hail, sovereign salve for sin full sore!
To thee all bows
Hail, lovely Lord, all care may cure!
Hail, King of Jews!

CHILDREN.
Hail, diamond, born and burnished bright!
Hail, gentle jasper of Jewry!
Hail, lily lovesome, leamed with light!
Hail, help and healing from on high

A CAPELLA – SEMICHOR.
Hail, conqueror, hail, most of might!
Hail, ransomer of sinners all!
Hail, merciful! Hail, holy light!
Hail, that shall raise us when we fall!

OMNES.
Hail, dreadful judge that all shall doom!
Hail, quick and dead, that none may doubt!
Hail, thou that worship best becomes!
Hail, Lord, whose laws no man may flout!
We welcome thee.
Hail, and be welcome of all about
To our city.

End of First Part.

Interval.

PART TWO

26. Cutlers

PILATE *on his tribunal with two other* ROMAN
MAGISTRATES. *Enter* CAIAPHAS, ANNAS, LAWYERS,
PRIESTS, KNIGHTS, ROMAN SOLDIERS.

PILATE.

Pons Pilate am I
A Prince parlous and proud
Let him shudder and blench
That my judgement shall blame,
For his life he shall lack
Or his limbs I shall lop
Who no low bow will make,
Nor who think'st not to stoop.

Regent most royal I rule this roost
Canopied here in my solemn state –
Come, sirs – tell me, if ye would'st,
What grievance, gripe, or sharp debate
D'ye bring to judgement hot and just? –
Since in my hands hangs all men's fate.

ANNAS.

O, sir, there is a troublesome swain
Whose rule is not right.
Reports of him through this domain
Raise tumult and fright.

PILATE.

Yea? This Jesus?
I know how ye hate him.
Your hearts will not peace.
Unless I abate him –
Mischief will increase.
But why bay ye so furious fierce?
Be calm, and your reasons array.

CAIAPHAS.
> To our people, sir, treason he teaches.

ANNAS.
> We seek for your succour today.

PILATE.
> But be his teachings lawful? Allege not too long
> For we may, if we please, let him preach with good will.

ANNAS.
> Then we fail of a friend, and our people have wrong –
> If, thus, this false felon your favour saves still.

PILATE *makes gesture of dismissal*.

CAIAPHAS.
> Sir!
> The unrest he stirs up is curst, and so strong
> He must shortly be shent ere our ruin befall.
> For he teaches the people to call him 'God's son'.

OMNES JEWS.
> O shame! –

ANNAS.
> That this fellow speaks free is a shame on us all!
> For he says he soon shall take his seat
> In Highest Heaven – his rightful estate.

PILATE.
> It seems ye will not make an end –
> But is he that Christ ye say should descend
> Both ye and your children to save?

CAIAPHAS.
> Ah, soft, sir.
> For of Christ when he comes no kin shall be known
> But of this caitiff's kin we know every last one.
> Though he claims like great God everlasting to be –
> To lift up the laden – to slay, or to free.

PILATE.
> To hurt him now is all your note,
> But yet the law lies in my lot –

ANNAS.

    Sir, when in our Temple he taught
    Where tables of treasure all lay
    He cast them down – that caitiff! –
    And counted it naught –

CAIAPHAS.

    O, is this not perjury to print under pen?
    Why save an apostate, sir? Pray you, sir, bend.

PILATE.

    What intend ye?

CAIAPHAS.

    To do him to death, sir, for disturbing of men.

PILATE.

    Then 'twould be *your* mastery, made him to mourn?
    It shall not be so, sirs. This court's at an end –

Rising. The two MAGISTRATES *rise with him.*

CAIAPHAS.

    But, sir, on our sabbath the sick would he save
    Nor cease, at our bidding, to sink into sin –

ANNAS.

    He holds not our holy day – hard hap may he have! –
    Let him stretch forth his neck –

PILATE.

                    How now, sir? Rein in!
    What? Ye'd ride roughshod the guiltless to his grave?
    Groundless, ye'll gain naught such grief to begin.
    So look that ye bear witness true –
    And without any trifles to tell.

ANNAS.

    Truth certain, our sayings we seal.

CAIAPHAS.

    O sir, were his faults not so fell
    We would not have meddled at all.
    He seduces our people to approve of his preaching –
    On that point you should press him, his power to impair –

FIRST DOCTOR.
  Yea, sir – and worse, sir – he calls him our king –

PILATE.
  What!

SECOND DOCTOR.
  For which cause our people are cast into care.

PILATE.
  King? King! If true, that boast his bale will bring
  And make him ban bitter the bones he bares –
  Such a wretch from our wrath shall not wing
  Ere wrack be wrought upon him –

OMNES JEWS.
  So would we it were!

  PILATE *confers with* CAIAPHAS *and* ANNAS, JUDAS
  comes to PILATE's *gate.*

JUDAS
  Ingenti pro inuria – Him – Jesus – that Jew!
  Unjust to me, Judas. His lordship I loathe…
  'Twas at supper we sat – if you'd know the whole truth –
  With Simon the Leper – when my schemes came to grief.
  Some woman brought a box – that was cause of my woe! –
  And fell at his feet, bowing low, by my troth –
  Then she smears 'em with ointment – rare, precious and new.
  For the waste of that worth I wax wondrous wrath.
  And what was my reason? Then know:
  Of all his pence I purser was
  And 'twas my trick to sneak his wealth
  A tenth of everything he got
  I'd steal and spend upon myself.
  But since I'm now cheat of my share
  Let him of my revenge beware.
  'That ointment precious,' I said, 'that stuff might be sold
  For as much as three hundred in bright silver pence
  And shared out among all the poor and the old' –
  Though for poor and for old – well, I couldn't care less –
  No, what troubled me more was the loss of my tenth.
  Now right quick I hence will flit
  To Caiaphas of priests our prince,

Sell him my master – and so get,
Again, my missing thirty pence.

In this way shall he
Learn what it means
Thus to cheat me.

Ho, porter! Open the ports of this proud place.

PORTER (*a Roman soldier*).
Glowering gadling! Take hence your scabby face.

JUDAS.
I have secrets to sell.

PORTER.
Yea, some treasons to tell –
Say, beetle-browed briber why blow'st'yow such boasts?

JUDAS.
No malice I mean, sir, but come in I must.

PORTER.
Say'st thou – unhanged harlot? The devil thee rend!
Thou looks't like a lumpkin whose livelihood's lost –
Woe shall I work thee if thou will not wend!

JUDAS.
But tidings full true I can tell!
Through my news, from dire dangers your masters may 'scape
Let me in and they'll say you've done well.

PORTER.
Bide here, then, bold braggart.

He goes to PILATE.

My lord, thou source of wisdom's well,
I come, in care, a case to lay.

PILATE.
Aha! Speak on – spare not thy spell.

CAIAPHAS.
We'll meddle too then, if we may.

PORTER.
Well, sir, in short then, there stands at your gate
A hind, hilt-full of ire, and hasty in hate.

CAIAPHAS.
What's he want?

PORTER.
I've no idea.
He's clad in a cloak – wrapped around him – like this –
And he got a face on him a pig wouldn't kiss.

CAIAPHAS.
Go fetch him.

JUDAS.
May all the gods, sir, sustain your renown –

ANNAS.
You'd better kneel down.

PILATE.
Welcome.

CAIAPHAS.
Now what's your game?

PILATE.
Come now, speak to me. Have no fear.

JUDAS.
I'd break a bargain to ye, much mischief to mar.
My cause, sirs, is great, let me tell you.
For if ye will bargain and buy
One – Jesus – right soon will I sell you.

OMNES.
Ah!

ANNAS.
Blessing, dear son, shall'ee win thereby!

PILATE.
What's your name?

JUDAS.
Judas Iscariot.

ANNAS.
Clearly, a good man!

PILATE.
Then Jesus before us shall fairly be tried.

CAIAPHAS.
But bid now your bargain. What would ye? Say.

JUDAS.
Thirty pence – not a penny more, not a penny less –
Thus am I paid.

ANNAS.
Now, Judas, I warn ye, our plots don't betray –
For treachery, the devil would fetch thee away.

CAIAPHAS.
Some trick must thou teach on your master to make
Or away with a warning the fellow will fly.

JUDAS.
I shall show you a token him tite for to take
When he's thringing in throng – O there'll be no escape!

SOLDIER.
How shall we know him?

JUDAS.
He's the one I shall kiss…

PILATE.
Then this bargain is made. Kneel down – and take this.
It's thy silver. Take it up. Away now – it's done
Much joy may it bring ye! (*Throwing it down.*)

JUDAS.
Yea! My great grief is gone.

SOLDIER.
(*Aside to* JUDAS.) Be light, then. It will buy a rope to
hang ye.

JUDAS.
I'll deliver his corse in care you to clap.

ANNAS.
More comfort in this case we nor covet nor crave.

SOLDIER.
When we catch that rascal his ribs will we rap
Yea, that rogue, ere I rest, will be running to rave.

PILATE.
>Yet if he be blameless, it behoves us to save.
>So, sir, if ye beat him, then spoil not his shape.

SOLDIER.
>All we'll do is make sure, sir, he shall not escape
>So soon in your sight, sir, we'll set him.

CAIAPHAS.
>Good lad. Now flit forth. Go and get him.

>*Here should follow the mime of the Last Supper, then out
>to Gethsemane.*

28. Cordwainers

JESUS.
>Behold, my disciples in dignity dear,
>How I shudder and shrink for doubt of my deed.
>Mine enemies encompass me – drawing full near –
>With what might they may muster to mar my manhood.

>But since ye are o'erwatched – and wandered far in fear –
>Look ye, set down and rest – this I bid.
>Be not heavy of your hearts, but stay even here
>And bide by me a brief while, here in this stead.

>Be watchful and wise in your resting –
>See that ye be wakeful alway
>And look that ye cease not to pray
>To my Father for strength never failing.

PETER.
>Yea, Lord. At thy bidding
>Obedient we here abide.

JOHN.
>Lord, our help at your needing
>We mean not to hide.

>*JESUS goes off a little way.*

JAMES.

    What way is he wand'ring
    In all this world wide?

They kneel and pray but soon fall asleep.

JESUS.

    Restore and renew me
    With voice sure and calm
    Thou healer of harm
    And builder of bliss.
    As thou art balm of all sorrows
    And all help and health in thy hands has,
    Maintain now my courage –
    Mend all that's amiss.

    Oh, if it be possible, let this pain overpass.
    Yet – Father – if thou see'st it may not –
    Even at thine own will
    Be it worthily wrought
    Both mildly and still
    And with patience endured.

    Unto my disciples will I wend again,
    Kindly to comfort them. In care they are caught.
    What! Are ye fallen asleep now – every one?
    My Passion ye have in your minds no more –
    Would ye leave me thus lightly to suffer alone
    Abandoned to sorrows, a captive to care?
    To whom may I move me and make now my moan?
    Come! Peter – all – wake up! How should this be?
    Art thou so strongly oppressed by this power?
    Might ye not – the space of one short hour –
    Have watched and prayed for me?

PETER.

    Forgive us, Lord.

JESUS.

    Fail me not.
    Be watchful, and pray, while ye stay here,
    To our Father, though tempted ye fall not –
    For great evil draws near.

JESUS *withdraws to pray.* DISCIPLES *make great efforts to stay awake but fall asleep.*

O, Father that formed all, my flesh would full fain
Be turned from this torment and returned unto thee,
For mazed is my manhood in mood and in main
But if thou, who sees't all, require it of me –
That Thy son, for man's sin, shall be innocent slain –
Be it worthily wrought... At Thy will let it be –
For I bow to Thy bidding, and obedient remain.

He goes back to the DISCIPLES.

Yea, sleep ye so fast? All for weariness bend?
Then sleep while ye may, I shall let you alone.
I fear ye for frailty are failing your friend.
I'll unto my prayers and my sorrows return.

Oh Father, if I must death taste
At Thy will I shall bend.
Though my flesh must fail, Father, I am fain
That mine anguish and suffering be soon brought to end.

GABRIEL, MICHAEL *and the other* ARCHANGELS *and* ANGELS *appear. They comfort and strengthen him. Then he goes again to the* DISCIPLES.

Sleep ye all safely now? Soon must I be taken
With treason and pain – by each of you forsaken –

PETER.
Nay, soothly, I'll never my sovereign forsake
Though here, for the deed, I dreadfully die –

JOHN.
Such a lout of me shall never man make.
I would die first –

JAMES.
In faith, so should I!

JESUS.
Yea?
But when that time befalls that men shall me take
Like sheep from the wolf away ye shall make –

PETER.

> Nay, soothly! – For while I may avail thee
> Never, for faint-heart, shall I fail thee.

JESUS.

> Ah, Peter...
> Of such boasting – I warn thee – let be.
> For all thy protesting, full keenly I know
> In fear of my foes thou shalt soon me deny –
> Three times and throughly before the cock crow.

> *Enter* JUDAS *with* ANNAS, *the* KNIGHTS *and* TEMPLE
> GUARD. *Some have flaming torches.*

JUDAS.

> All hail, Master, in faith, and all fellows here.

JESUS.

> Now is the hour drawing full near
> That will certify sooth of all I have said.

JUDAS.

> With greeting most gracious this ground be arrayed.
> I would ask a kiss of you, Master, if your will it were
> For my love and my liking upon you is laid.

JESUS.

> With all my heart, Judas, take it even here –
> Thus, with a kiss, the Son of Man is betrayed.

FIRST KNIGHT.

> Ho! Stand, traitor! I tell thee thou'rt ta'en.

ANNAS.

> On, on, knights! Go fall on before.

> *A brilliant light shines from* JESUS *which half-blinds
> the enemies.*

THIRD KNIGHT.

> Alas we are lost through gleam of this flame!

JESUS.

> Say, whom do ye seek? What would you? Say?

MALCHUS.

> One Jesus of Nazareth – that traitor I name.

JESUS.

Behold – here I stand. Why seek ye me?

MALCHUS.

To take thee to trial, dastard, since it is thou –

PETER.

Stand off, by my faith or thy foul fell I'll flay –
That for thee, braggart – what say ye now!

Cuts off MALCHUS' *ear*.

MALCHUS.

Ow! I say ow! What d'ye do that for?

PETER *slashes at him again*.

JESUS.

Peace, Peter! Patience I bid thee.
Meddle not, nor move thee no more
For – wit ye all well – if my will it were –
I have angels in legions to save and defend me.
Strike not again.
He that loves vengeance – vengeance be his reward –
Vengeance feeds vengeance and pain breeds from pain.
Put up your sword.

Be calm. Young man, come here.
I shall thee heal.

MALCHUS.

But he's cut off my ear!
It'll never be whole!

JESUS *heals* MALCHUS, *who is amazed*.

ANNAS.

Now, soldiers, now! Pile on, every one –
Let's lay on this lad – get a grip if you can.

The SOLDIERS *fall on* JESUS. DISCIPLES *flee*. JOHN
runs away naked.

JESUS.

I taught daily in your Temple. Why took ye me not there?
Now darkness on Earth hath the height of his power.

ANNAS.
Keep fast hold of the lurdan and bind him in bands.

MALCHUS.
Well done, fellows – yes – by my faith he is fast.

FIRST KNIGHT.
We have a hard hold of this hawk in our hands.

MALCHUS.
And unto Sir Caiaphas we'll lug him at last.

Exit triumphant with noise.

29. Bowyers and Fletchers

Enter CAIAPHAS, *from a good dinner, a little drunk,*
with GUARDS *and* ATTENDANTS, *on his way to bed.*

SERVANT.
Now come, lord, to your rest –
The day is close at hand –
Some wine to slake your thirst?
I warrant ye shall find
There'll be tidings right soon.
To bed, now. Away.

CAIAPHAS.
Bring me wines of the best
For the more that I booze
Then the better I'll rest.

MALCHUS.
My lord! My lord! My lord! Here's a lark if ye list!

CAIAPHAS.
Leave off, jackanapes! Less noise!

MALCHUS.
My lord, it is the news that ye wished.

Enter ANNAS *in a hurry.*

CAIAPHAS.
What? Is that Jesus found?

MALCHUS.

Yea, they're bringing him here, guarded and bound.

JESUS *is brought in*.

ANNAS.

Say, lad, will ye not bow to your lord?

MALCHUS.

Not him, sir –

FIRST KNIGHT.

By your leave we shall teach him to stoop in this place –

CAIAPHAS.

Nay, nay, sir – not so. Let's do nothing in haste –
It's no fun beating beasts that are bound.
First, in fairness and justice the truth we shall taste
Then spare him or smite as we've found.
Now loose him, and leave us – go get ye all gone.
Sir Annas and I shall try him alone.

SOLDIERS *go, except* FIRST KNIGHT.

Of the friends that have feed thee, speak fellow…
Now come!
Speak frankly and freely – Say, who set you on?

MALCHUS.

I told you – He's dumb.

FIRST KNIGHT.

And Malchus this man, lord, that had his ear shorn
This harlot hath healed it by help of Mahoun.

CAIAPHAS.

What! Did he? If the lad means to do good
Let him hear how we'll hasten to urge him.

ANNAS.

Nay – by Beelzebub's bones and his blood
I believe it's much better to scourge him –

CAIAPHAS.

Nay, soft, sir – less haste…
Boy, be never aghast if we seem so gay
I conjure thee kindly and command thee also,

By great God who liveth and reigneth on high –
If thou be God's son – called the Christ – tell us so.

JESUS.

As thou say'st thyself, and truly I say
That I go to my Father – He I came fro –
To dwell joyful with Him and in weal alway –

ANNAS.

Why, fie on thee, faithless! False heart and untrue!
Thy God hast thou foully defamed –
What need we further his offences to view
When he with the words of his own mouth is shamed?

CAIAPHAS.

What further witnesses need we to call? –
He stands here condemnèd by what he hath said.

ANNAS.

He slanders the Godhead and sore grieves us all –
I deem and I doom he deserves to be dead –

CAIAPHAS.

– And he shall!
Sure he shall!
D'ye hear me, young harlot? Ill hap on your head!
Answer us straightway – your lords here in hall –
And reach us some reasons right sharp as I bid.

JESUS.

My reasons from you are hid.
Nor those who would help me – I would not them call.
I say alway the sooth – yet will ye not assent
But hinder, or haste me to hang.
I preach where the people were ever most present
And never in privity nor to old nor to young.
Also, in your Temple I told my intent –
Ye might have taken me there for my teaching.
Much better to bring me with brands all unbrent
Than to take me by night, all for nothing –

CAIAPHAS.

For nothing! Nothing! False blasphemer, you lie! –

JESUS.

> Sir, since thou with wrongs seek'st to turn me awry,
> Go ask them that heard of my speaking –

CAIAPHAS.

> Ah! This traitor torments me – What tales hath he told!
> I had ne'er from such harlot as he so much scorn!

Rages, and tears his own robes.

FIRST KNIGHT.

> What! Shame on thee, beggar! Who made thee so bold?
> (*Strikes* JESUS.)
> Bandy looks with our bishop, lad? – I'll be thy bane!

CAIAPHAS.

> Pick him up – Ding him down –
> Let him hang for this shame!

KNIGHTS *return.*

ANNAS.

> Sir, remember we're churchmen!

Abashed. They are not sure how to proceed.

CAIAPHAS.

> We must seem free of blame.

ANNAS.

> Then let's send him to Pilate,
> Demanding his doom,
> For Pilate is judge here, and viceroy on high –
> Only right that a Roman should doom him to die.

CAIAPHAS.

> Well said, sir, and cunning, and so it shall be.
> Now, my knights, teach yon boy there 'tis better to bow.

FIRST KNIGHT.

> I shall learn him, my lord, if you'll leave him to me,
> To bend low to lords – And he'll learn fast I trow.

THIRD KNIGHT.

> Now crack on, one and all. And there's one! (*Striking him.*)

FIRST KNIGHT.

> And there's two! – Give him each a sound slap –

SECOND KNIGHT.
    And there's three!

FOURTH KNIGHT.
    And there's four!

THIRD KNIGHT.
    Now tell us, young chap,
    Who's smacking thee now? Can you not prophesy?
    Say who was it – who?

FIRST KNIGHT.
    What – never a word, lad? You've nowt to say now?

CAIAPHAS.
    Hurry. Take him to Pilate, we'll unto him plain –
    Say that this lad with his lies hath our laws laughed to scorn
    Well demand that this same day the boy must be slain
    Because that our sabbath begins the next morn. (*Exeunt.*)

    Outside in the courtyard. There are SOLDIERS *around a fire.*
    Enter a WOMAN *with empty wine jug, etc., from*
    CAIAPHAS's *room. She sees* PETER, *trying to warm himself.*

WOMAN.
    Out, caitiff! Who says thou may stand
    So silent and sullen and lost in thy thought?
    Thy master has wrought mickle wrong in this land –
    That jester – that Jesus – that flaunter of law!

PETER.
    Peace, woman, you're wasting your words and your wind
    For of his company ne'er was I kenned.

    Enter JESUS *under guard, unseen by* PETER *and the*
    WOMAN.

WOMAN.
    You deny here the sayings he said?
    That we should all call him God's son –
    And while he was with us in't world
    His bidding should always be done?

PETER.
    I must partake of your prattle. What can I say more?
    For women are windbags – it's bred in the bone –

This man that you speak of I never once saw
And one of his fellowship never was none.

MALCHUS.
Look, knights, look here – Come and take heed –
That's the boy with his brand what brayed me full near
When we took this man that in bands we have brought
He nimbly and naughtily nipped off my ear –

PETER.
I was never with him in aught that he wrought –
Nor in word nor in work, nor in thought nor in deed!

Cock crows.

JESUS.
You said you would my comfort be
In weal or woe, in sorrow and care.
Peter, remember what ere I said
That thrice hath now forsaken me.

PETER.
Alack the day that I came here! –
Or e'er denied my Lord apart –
The sadness on his face full clear
Hath seared my soul and broke my heart.

30. Tapiters and Couchers

PILATE*'s ornate, well-furnished bedroom, before dawn.*
PILATE *in bed.*

DAME PERCULA.
I am Dame Precious Percula, of princes the prize,
Wife to Sir Pilate there, prince without peer,
Mirror of womanhood, witty and wise –
Observe well my countenance, comely and clear,
Firm, and fair of figure… and small in size.
No lord in this land – I'd stake my life –
Is more fortunate in his choice of wife
Than you, my dear, though I say it myself
That shouldn't –

PILATE.
    Then I'll say it too. Who wouldn't?

PERCULA.
    Go on then – say it again.

PILATE.
    My body's in flames – I must kiss you, my dame.

PERCULA.
    To arouse your desires, oh my fair lord, I'm fain.

PILATE.
    Lovely lips made for kisses – in bed we'll remain.

PERCULA.
    For kissing and fondling and… that I'll not name –

    Enter the BEADLE *– a young man – suddenly.*

BEADLE.
    My liberal lord, O leader of laws,
    As you are judge and justice of Jews –

PERCULA.
    Not now! Go away! Wretched boy!

BEADLE.
    But, Madame, I am only doing my job –

PILATE.
    Nay, calm yourself, Madame be patient I pray
    For I fear it's our duty to hear what he'll say.

BEADLE.
    Quick, get up, sir – sleep no more
    The Council's waiting at the door –

    DAME PERCULA *rushes off, clad in a sheet.*

PILATE.
    What Council? Not those churchmen?

BEADLE.
    Yes, sir. The whole pack and chapter of them.

PILATE.
    Now Great Caesar shield us!

He gets up and washes and dresses. LUCIFER *appears.*

LUCIFER.

Hell's sovereignty hangs by a thread –
I may lose everything I've won?
For if God's Son at last be slain
Then by his death great power he'll gain –
Conquer my kingdom and clatter my crown –
Succour Man's soul saved from Hell's sharp pain –
Sure, I shall go down.
If I'm to survive,
I must keep Jesus alive.

To accomplish great evil one must seem to do good.
My plots all need women – I've got one to hand –
Sir Pilate's witless wife – she's both stubborn and proud
And by telling one truth, all truth I'll undermine.

O woman be wary and wise, and awaken thy wit,
(*Whispering in her ear.*)
Before thy husband, in bands, by harlot bishops brought
Jesus, that gentle man, stands sore beset
And today, to his death must, guiltless, be dight.
Your husband, by bending his mastery to these Jews,
Needs must all his fortune lay low – and yours.

Exit LUCIFER. DAME PERCULA *wakes.*

PERCULA.

Boy! Go, boy, to your master and tell him from me
That I dreamed of one Jesus, the Jews would undo –
With tricks they would trap him – he must be set free –
Go beg that my husband let this good man go.

BEADLE.

Madame, in haste, I shall run and say so.

Exit BEADLE.

CAIAPHAS.

Good morrow, my sovereign.

PILATE.

Come in, both of you. To the bench we'll make haste.

CAIAPHAS.

Nay, not so, good sir. Lower is lawful for us.

PILATE.

Ah, sir, Caiaphas, in courtesy, give way ye must.

ANNAS.

Now, nay, my good lord – nay, it must not be thus –

PILATE.

Speak no more – sit beside me. I won't be opposed.

PILATE, CAIAPHAS, and ANNAS mount the Tribunal.
Enter BEADLE.

BEADLE

Sir, your wife commends her to you
And says that this morn she lay long in her bed
With sorrow, with troubles, and with much ado
For a dream that swept swiftly and strange to her head
Of one Jesus – a just man – the Jews would undo...
She beseeches, good sir, set the innocent free,
From death be his shield, lest God's vengeance fall quick –

PILATE.

What? Is this that same Jesus you've haled before me?

CAIAPHAS.

Pay no heed to this trick
For 'tis surely with witchcraft your wife he hath wrought.
Some fiend, with these dreams, it would seem, he hath sent –

ANNAS.

This is certain and sure and the truth should be sought.
He worked many such wonders wherever he went
And we say, for such fiendcraft, his death he hath bought –

PILATE.

Not so fast.
Be ye never so fierce. Ye must both abide
Until such a traitor be proved for untrue.
Go, boy, and bring him straight to my side –
If he be just, he shall not need to rue...
(*Aside*.) His plight hath touched me to the heart...

BEADLE.

(*To* JESUS.) Now, Jesus, your judges these priests of
     their hate
Bid me bring you before them, all bound up in bands,

Yon lords lust for thy downfall – their rage to abate –
But here I thee worship with heart and with hands.
(*Kneels asking for blessing.*)
This reverence to thee I bring
Whom ever hath worshipped full hallowed on high –

KNIGHTS *drag him to his feet.*

ANNAS.
Now, in your sight, sir, the sooth I shall say –
As you are a prince, take good note now, I pray,
This liar and traitor, my life I dare lay,
Many folk of this land would lead lewdly astray –

BEADLE *makes as if to protest.* ANNAS *clouts him.*

PILATE.
Speak, boy, who gave thee leave to bow low to yon lad?
And solace him seemly in my sight, as I saw?

BEADLE.
Oh Master lour not, for many do as I have done
Great men spread rich robes at his feet
And poor folk fetch flowers, fresh and sweet,
In him there was never harm.

PILATE.
Now, seigneurs, speak you – is what the lad says right?

CAIAPHAS.
Nay, lord, this lad is too lewd, by this light.
If his statements were searched and by lawyers assayed –
It soon should be proved that this simpleton lied.

BEADLE.
The lies are not mine – only truth have I told.

ANNAS.
And I say, light harlot, your tongue ye shall hold! –
And nought 'gainst thy masters speak thus.

PILATE.
Cease now your squabbling. I'll search him full sore.

ANNAS.
Nay, doom him to death, sir – Let him have law!

PILATE.

Sir, have you finished?

ANNAS.

Yea, lord…

PILATE.

Then sit you down soberly, there on the bench.
I will do him no harm that hath done no offence.
Now, Jesus, believe me, right welcome you are.
Be not afraid, come ye here to the bar.
Now, prelates, your charges be proving –
What case can ye make to accuse him?

CAIAPHAS.

Sir, Pontius Pilate, peerless prince of great price
We trow ye will trust all our tales to be true
And doom him to death now with all due device.

PILATE.

Your tales I might trust if your case ye can prove.

CAIAPHAS.

Sir, halt men and lame he hath healed of their hurts
The deaf and the dumb he delivered from dole
By witchcraft, I'll warrant, his wonders he works
And in awe of these wonders, men follow this fool.

PILATE.

Then, tell me, sirs – what would ye have me say?

CAIAPHAS.

Sir, doom him directly – He must die this day.

PILATE.

So… Because he does good, with his life he must pay?
Go, go! Are ye larking? Who learned ye your law?
This is no treason, ye told me.

ANNAS.

                              Then list well, ye –
Yon briber, right boldly, bids all to forbear
Our taxes to Caesar. Now how say ye, sir?

PILATE.

If treasons to Caesar be proven, he dies.
But first I will hear for myself what he says.

Speak, Jesu, and pray thou thy answers may speed.
These lordings allege thou liv'st not by their laws –
They accuse thee full cruel and keen...
And therefore as viceroy I charge thee:
If thou be Christ, tell me –
For this is the matter they mean.

JESUS.
Thou sayest so thyself – I am soothly the same
Here wending in world, to work all my will.
My Father in Heaven – I come in his name.
With nor trespass nor sin am I brought ye until.

PILATE.
Lo, bishops, why blame ye this boy?
Me seems it is sooth that he says –
Why move all the malice ye may
With your cunning and wiles to wrench him awry? –
Thus unjustly to judge him from joy.

ANNAS.
In this felon ye favour, great faults we can find
And this day ye must doom him to die –

PILATE.
'Must', sir, 'Must'? That's false, by this light!
Would'st preach at me, ribald? Thou reckons not right!

ANNAS.
Sir, wreak not your wrath now on me.
Advise you, sir, with main and might –

PILATE.
I like not your language – I warn you take heed –

CAIAPHAS.
Ah, mercy, lord – meekly – we speak not in spite –

PILATE.
Then answer me, bishops, how came he so wise?

CAIAPHAS.
In truth, Prince of Men, that is hid from our eyes.

PILATE.
Then mean ye from malice to thwart him by force? –

Of crimes to convict him, though all without cause?
I marvel ye aim so amiss.

CAIAPHAS.

From Galilee, sir, he continues his course
And stirs up our people to flout all our laws
And to this we bear witness, iwis.

PILATE.

What? From Galilee came he? – Ye gadabout lad!

CAIAPHAS.

From Galilee, sir – he was born there, and bred.

PILATE.

Then hale him to Herod – let him judge in my stead
For Herod is king there, as ye right well know,
Then take up our guest, sirs – to Herod he'll go
And say that the doom of this case I concede.
To that king I submit him to live or to bleed.

MALCHUS.

You heard what he said, lads, come on now, take heed.

KNIGHTS *lead* JESUS *away*.

32. Cooks and Waterleaders

JUDAS.

Ah weladay that I was wrought! –
Or ever I came by kind or kin –
I curse the bones that forth me brought!
Woe on the womb that I bred in!
So must I bid
For I so falsely dealt with him
That unto me all kindness did.
There was none he trusted so well as I –
I that betrayed him traitorly –
With lies all vain.
Blameless I bartered his blest body
Unto Jews to be slain.

CAIAPHAS.
> What tidings, Judas? You here again?

JUDAS.
> Sir, I have sinned full grievously –
> Betrayed my righteous Lord – Jesus –
> True master mine –

ANNAS.
> What's that to us?
> The sin is thine.

JUDAS.
> And of that sin I here repent!
> If ye assent my Lord to slay –

CAIAPHAS.
> What can I do? What's your intent?

JUDAS.
> I beg ye, bishop, set him free
> And here take back your payment plain.

CAIAPHAS.
> Nay, nay, thou fool, it may not be –

ANNAS.
> We bought him that he might be slain.

> JUDAS *throws down the silver coins.*

CAIAPHAS.
> What the devil's wrong with you?
> When first thou sought us thou wast full fain
> Of this money. What ails thee now?

JUDAS.
> Oh take it again!
> I curse my wickedness and guilt
> So great my sin in grisly guise
> I wax in woe he should be spilt
> And might I save him in any wise –
> Joy for me then!
> Save him, sir, and you I'll serve –
> Ever bound your bondsman to be.
> Lord Bishop, this good man's life preserve
> And I shall ever faithful be!

ANNAS.
>Faithful? Thee? Ill hap on ye fall!
>By Mahoun's blood! – Ye'd sell us all!

Exeunt CAIAPHAS *and* ANNAS.

JUDAS.
>My life, then, I loathe. Too long I have lived.
>My traitorly trick bought me nothing but pain
>And since taint of my treason may not be forgiven
>I ask for no mercy, for I've deserved none.
>Alas, who may I plain unto?
>Worthless, my words are wasted breath
>My life at last I will fordo
>And haste away to hang myself.

Exit.

31. Lysterers

Enter HEROD ANTIPAS, *his* DUKES, *and his* COURT, *braying drums and trumpets, in barbaric procession, with the* KNIGHTS *who brought* JESUS *to him, and* JESUS *dressed in rich robes.*

HEROD ANTIPAS.
>Peace, ye brothels and brawls in this broad way embraced! –
>And make low obeisance in majesty's presence
>Greet royalty royally kneeling in silence
>Not jostling for places but ranked all in reverence...

They all treat JESUS *as a king, bowing low and mocking him.*

>Now hear this – our sentence:
>We find no fault in this man to defile
>Wherefore we should flay him or hang him.
>In the rolls of our law we find nothing at all. So –
>Since he seems dumb, to condemn him –
>Were not good lore for a lord right royal. As I am.
>Then back to Sir Pilate ye'll straightway repair
>We lend him our lordship to judge what is good.
>Let that Roman pass sentence – I'm not in the mood.

Thus girt in his goodly gear gay
Dance on in the Devil's way!

Exeunt, noise, rejoicing, laughter.

33. Tilemakers or Millers

MALCHUS.
Hail, loveliest lord that ever law led
Hail, seemliest sovereign on every side
Hail, most in might and stateliest in stead
Hail –

PILATE.
Yes, yes… What tidings this tide?

MALCHUS.
King Herod, sir – his lips, sir, were lame
For all his boasts would not condemn
But stood as dumb as a nail in door –
So sends him back all free of blame.

PILATE (*to the* COURT).
Sirs, now listen to me…
Ye hear what we have in hand.
King Herod, no fault in him found
For which this Jesus should die.
And so, sirs, say I…

ANNAS.
Thou, Jesus, descended from Duke Jacob's kin –
Nazareth ne'er-do-well – name I thy name –
All creatures accuse thee – I bid thee come in
To answer thine enemies. Fend now thy fame.

JESUS.
Each man hath a mouth, that moveth on mould,
In weal or in woe to wield at his will.
If he govern it goodly, as God wills he would
For speech of things spiritual, none should him spill.

But woe to the wight who uses words ill
For trifling with truth great evils shall hap

Each word of his mouth shall be counted until
There comes a great Judgment...
That – none may escape.

PILATE.

Hear that, sirs?
Proceed further and you're mad.
Of his words no deceit can you make
Nor find any just cause to punish the lad.

CAIAPHAS.

Know, it's not without cause, sir, we come to accuse,
We'd have you deal fairly, and judge in good faith.

PILATE.

Sirs, deaf to defence, ye would not hear the truth
Nor will not relent till ye drive him to death.
Then take him yourselves away
And as much as your laws give you leave
Do on his body all that ye may –

CAIAPHAS.

Nay!

OMNES JEWS

Nay!

ANNAS.

O, Sir Pilate, prince without peer, give way!
No, sir, you know, as does every man here,
We may not kill him – we have not the power.
In your hands lies the force of all law.

PILATE.

Yea. Nor shall I doom him who hath done no ill deed.
Here I grant, with good will, he shall wend on his way.

CAIAPHAS.

No, sir, he shall not – no – take ye heed!
To be king, he claimeth, with a crown –
And whoso boldly will challenge such state
You should deem, to be dinged down –
Struck dead.

PILATE.

Sir, truly that touches on treason

And therefore will I with good reason
Punish – ere I stir from this stead.
Sir Knights, bold and comely, take this caitiff in keeping
Skelp him with scourges and serve him full sore
Wrack him and wring him till for woe he be weeping
Then bring him back here to stand us before.

The KNIGHTS *drag* JESUS *away.*

FIRST KNIGHT.
Soon shall he curse the day he was born.
Now shall we serve him as ye have said.

ANNAS.
Come. Whip off these weeds he hath worn.

FIRST KNIGHT.
Don't meddle, sir – let us instead.
Have done.

They shove ANNAS *away.*

FOURTH KNIGHT.
Let us get off his gear. God grant him ill grace!

THIRD KNIGHT.
Rip them off right – lo, tear off his trashes.

SECOND KNIGHT.
Now bind him with cords.

THIRD KNIGHT.
                              I am keen in this case.

FOURTH KNIGHT.
And now he's fast bound he must bear all our bashes.

FIRST KNIGHT.
Leap to it, lordings, and lay on with lashes.
(*They flog* JESUS.)
And now, because he would call him our king
We'll crown him most kindly with briars and thorns.

SECOND KNIGHT.
Yea, but first all in purple we'll lap the lad's limbs
And when royally arrayed let us laugh him to scorn.

FIRST KNIGHT.

Now reach me a reed for his sceptre to serve
And – here – set him down on this stool for his throne.
Ave, roy royal and *rex judeorum*!

OMNES KNIGHTS.

Hail, comely king that no kingdom can claim!
Hail, coward commander that no man commands!
Hail, blameless braggart that all men now blame!

FOURTH KNIGHT.

Hail, liberal lording with no lands to lend.

THIRD KNIGHT.

Hail, fearless freak whom no man calls friend.

They drag JESUS *back before the* COURT.

PILATE.

Sirs, *Ecce Homo* –
Bound, and well beaten, and brought ye before.
I judge he shall suffer no more.
Your custom hath been to let go
Some felon to freedom this day –

CAIAPHAS.

Yea – Barrabas in prison lies low
At this feast now release him, we pray.

PILATE.

Barrabas? That murderer – would you him free?
Would ye not rather that I should release Jesus?

OMNES

Nay! Barrabas, we say!

PILATE.

Prithee peace!

OMNES

Barrabas release! Barrabas release!

PILATE.

Will ye cease!
Your howling and brawling brings shame on this place.
If Barrabas ye'd have me to free

For Jesus what have ye in mind?
Barrabas is guilty in highest degree
In Jesus no fault can I find.

ANNAS.

Do as we have said – let him die.

PILATE.

Nay, I'll beat him again, then unbind –

ANNAS.

I say if ye free him you're not Caesar's friend!
This Jesus ye must crucify!

OMNES.

Crucify! Crucify!

Uproar in court. KNIGHTS *threaten crowd.*

PILATE.

Then his blood be upon you, say I.

ANNAS.

Yea – his blood be upon us – and there make an end.

OMNES.

Crucify! Crucify!

BEADLE.

Lord, here is the water for which ye did send
Will ye wash while it still be warm?

PILATE.

Then set forth Barrabas unleashed from his bands
Let him wend on his way – free from harm.
And now, bear me witness, all ye that stand here...

Washes hands.

From the guilt of his blood I pronounce myself clear.
Hear my judgement on Jesus, all Jews in this stead:
Crucify him on cross, and on Calvary him kill,
I condemn him this day to die this same death.
Take him and do your will.

34. Shermens

Crowd assembles. Enter procession. JESUS *carrying cross led by* ROMAN SOLDIERS. FIRST SOLDIER *is a wise old trooper;* SECOND SOLDIER *a squaddie;* THIRD SOLDIER *a young lad. The crowd presses on the soldiers who have difficulty in making a way up the hill.*

JESUS.
　　Ye daughters of Jerusalem
　　See ye mourn no more for me
　　But think on what is foretold.
　　For yourselves ye shall mourn,
　　And for the children yet unborn
　　Of you – both old and young.
　　For sure, there shall come a day
　　That in sorrowing and sighing ye shall say
　　Unto these hills on high:
　　'Fall on us, mountains – cover us here –
　　Hide us and shield us from all that fell fear
　　Which on us soon shall light.'

JOHN.
　　Lady, your weeping grieves me sore.

MARY.
　　John, help me, now or nevermore,
　　That I to him may come.

FIRST SOLDIER.
　　　　　　　　Be gone!
　　What the devil makes them stay?
　　How long must we stand still?
　　Go! Get ye hence away –
　　I'the devil's name! – Get up that hill!

THIRD SOLDIER.
　　Poor boy for loss of blood he flags –
　　This cross, too great for him to drag,
　　Will lay him low, I swear.

SECOND SOLDIER.
　　See! Here comes a likely lad
　　Shall help his load to bear.

FIRST SOLDIER.
Sir, here's a boy that must be led –
With loss of blood he is half-dead –
So thou must carry this tree
And help bear it to Calvary.

SIMON OF CYRENE.
Good sirs, alas, that may not be
For such great haste have I
I may not stay –

FIRST SOLDIER.
Now by the might of great Mahoun
I say we ding this dastard down –

They manhandle SIMON.

SIMON OF CYRENE.
Hold, sirs! This is not wisely wrought –
To beat me, though I trespass naught.

FIRST SOLDIER.
Whatever you may say
This deed must in great haste be done
Our boy must be stone-dead by noon
And now 'tis near midday.

JESUS *looks at* SIMON.

SIMON OF CYRENE.
To carry his cross now I hold me glad
Even as ye would it were.

FIRST SOLDIER.
Look that our gear be ready made
To work when we get there.

The procession continues to Calvary where the SOLDIERS
set out their gear and make ready to crucify JESUS. *There
are two other crosses already on Calvary.*

Whip off his weeds at once – let's see.
Aha! This garment will do for me –
This too will suit me well.

SECOND SOLDIER.
Nay, not so fast – that cannot be

All must be shared among us three
And as the die shall fall.

THIRD SOLDIER.
Yea – if Sir Pilate hear of this
Our share will be right small.

SECOND SOLDIER.
Well go and blab then if ye list
Sir Pilate shan't take all.
He'll get his due and nothing more.

FIRST SOLDIER.
Nay, let them lie there on the floor
Until the deed be done.

Throwing down the garments.

35. Pinners and Painters

Enter to the other three, FOURTH SOLDIER, *the NCO.*

FOURTH SOLDIER.
Now, men. It will our wits defy
To do this job and get it right –
Ye know yourselves, as well as I,
How priests and leaders of the law
Decreed today this lad must die.

FIRST SOLDIER.
Yea, sir, their counsel well we know –
That's why we're here on Calvary.

SECOND SOLDIER.
Just tell us what we have to do
And we'll set to as soon as may be.

THIRD SOLDIER.
Time we got along.

FOURTH SOLDIER.
Now to this work we must pay heed
Or else it'll all go wrong.

FIRST SOLDIER.
To tell us us jobs there is no need –

THIRD SOLDIER.
I shall go get our gear with speed –
Ropes, hammers – nails, sharp and long.

FOURTH SOLDIER.
Then we may boldly do this deed
Come, boys, let's kill this traitor strong.

SECOND SOLDIER.
The cross on ground is firmly stayed
And bored e'en as it ought to be.

FOURTH SOLDIER.
Then look that the lad be lengthways laid
And measured up against his tree.

They ignore JESUS *and sort out their gear.*

JESUS.
Almighty God, my Father free
Let all these deeds be kept in mind,
Thou bade that I should willing be
For Adam's fall to be sore pined.
Here unto death I must pledge me
Forth from his sin to save mankind
And – above all – beseech I thee
That Man, for my sake, may favour find
So that his soul ye save
In bliss withouten end.
I nought else crave.

He lies on the cross, and stretches out his arms.
The SOLDIERS *still don't notice.*

FIRST SOLDIER.
D'ye hear that, lads? By Mahoun's blood! –
For Adam's kind is all his thought.

SECOND SOLDIER.
The warlock waxes worse than mad
Of his own death he dreadeth nought.

FOURTH SOLDIER.
(*Turning to* JESUS.) Have done, my boy, and make thee boun
And bend thy back unto this tree.

THIRD SOLDIER.
Lads, look! Himself hath laid him down
In length and breadth as he should be.

FOURTH SOLDIER.
Go fast and fetter him then, ye three...
And since he claimeth kingdom and crown
Lifted on high like a king he must be.

They get ropes, hammers and nails and start to fasten
JESUS *to the cross*. FOURTH SOLDIER *watches them*.

SECOND SOLDIER.
Stand back and give me room
Till his right hand be fast.

THIRD SOLDIER.
His left arm then is mine –
We'll see who works the best.

FIRST SOLDIER.
His legs at length then will I stretch
And even unto the bore them fetch.

They work industriously.

FOURTH SOLDIER.
Now, lads, say, goes it as we planned?
Strike on, strike hard and spare him nought.

They nail the right hand.

THIRD SOLDIER.
Here's a good nail will stiffly stand
Through bone and sinew it will go straight –

SECOND SOLDIER.
Our work goes well now –

THIRD SOLDIER.
Give us a hand.

They laugh at their own 'hand and foot' jokes.

FIRST SOLDIER.
>Nay. It fails by a foot or more – just wait –
>See. The sinews are all done in.

SOLDIER TWO.
>I think your mark was wrongly scored.

FOURTH SOLDIER.
>Why carp ye? Fasten on a cord
>And stretch him till he reach the pin.

FIRST SOLDIER.
>Yea? Who d'ye think you are? A lord?
>Come help to stretch him then.

SECOND SOLDIER.
>That's what he was just about to do –

THIRD SOLDIER.
>As swift as any snail –

>*They stretch the left arm.*

>Now I can tack him all't way through –
>Hold tight while I whack in this nail.

>*He nails the other hand.*

FOURTH SOLDIER.
>Right. Now let's get hold his feet
>So he's fixed firm at the top and the tail.

SECOND SOLDIER.
>Heave!

FIRST SOLDIER.
>Haul!

FOURTH SOLDIER.
>Now hold him well –

SECOND SOLDIER.
>Heave!

FIRST SOLDIER.
>Haul!

THIRD SOLDIER.
Now I'll knock in my nail –

FOURTH SOLDIER.
Well done, us all…

They admire their work.

There yet remains another thing
That falls to ye and me
Our lords bid us that he should hang
On high for all to see.

They all grumble and set about lifting up the cross.

THIRD SOLDIER.
Be quick! This cross I must set down
Else break my back asunder soon.

FOURTH SOLDIER.
Set down, then. Leave your din.

They put down the cross and rest for a moment.

Right. Let's try again.
Lift hard and he shall soon be there.
Watch your fingers – hold it fast.

THIRD SOLDIER.
Oh lift!

FIRST SOLDIER.
We do!

FOURTH SOLDIER.
A little more.

THIRD SOLDIER.
I'm sore.

SECOND SOLDIER.
Hold then.

FOURTH SOLDIER.
Come, men!

FIRST SOLDIER.
How's that?

FOURTH SOLDIER.
The worst is past.

THIRD SOLDIER.
He's a wicked weight.

The cross is now upright.

FIRST SOLDIER.
So our bishops state.

The cross drops into its hole.

THIRD SOLDIER.
Methinks this cross will not abide
It sways there in the mortice yet.

SECOND SOLDIER.
I told you't hole were far too wide – (*Shakes the cross.*)
That makes it wobble – there! – see that?

FIRST SOLDIER.
Let's whack all in these wedges then
That should make our slack work fit.

They knock in wedges.

FOURTH SOLDIER.
(*To* JESUS.) Say, sir, do you approve
Our workmanship – what do you think?

THIRD SOLDIER.
Are you all right up there? –
Do ye feel faint? Could you do with a drink?

JESUS.
All men that see me hanging here
Write my misfortune on your hearts
Behold my head, my hands, my feet
And deeply feel ere ye depart
To mourn for me – may it be meet?
Forgive these wights that would me pine,
Father, they work they know not what,
But take their souls as thou hast mine
And of their sin think ye no thought.

FIRST SOLDIER.
> Now, sirs, I'll strike another note
> This garment must I of you crave.

SECOND SOLDIER.
> Nay, nay, sir, we will try by lot
> Which of us four his coat shall have.

THIRD SOLDIER.
> I say we should draw straws for it
> It's easy done – all quarrels to save...

FOURTH SOLDIER.
> Your wasting your breath, lad,
> This mantle I'll have.

Goes off with it.

FIRST SOLDIER.
> So much for fair play.

THIRD SOLDIER.
> I never wanted it anyway.

36. Butchers

JESUS.
> Hard-hearted man how can ye bear
> To see your maker hanging here?
> On the rood I am raggèd and rent –
> O, sinful soul – all for thy care.
> For thy misdeeds my life is spent
> My body broken, bowed, and bent.
> Who greater love of ye hath shown
> Than I?
> Thus for thy good
> I shed my blood
> Man, mend thy mood.
> In bitterness, eternal bliss
> For thee I buy.

ANNAS.
> Lord Pilate, pray take my advice

And wipe ye yon writing away
It says he is King of us Jews –
Write, rather, that title he claimed.

PILATE.

Quod scripsi, scripsi –
'Is King' wrote I.
I bide thereby.
However ye carp and complain.

CAIAPHAS.

By Mahoun! –
Thou'd'st save mankind from sin, ye said
To save thyself now let us see
And if thou be God's son indeed
Let's watch thee climb down off that tree
Right soon!

MARY.

Alas! Why must we part in twain?
My comfort is all turned to pain
Evermore.

JESUS.

Now, Mother list – instead of me
Take ye John, your son to be.
Endure.

For foxes their dens have they
Birds have they their nests
But the Son of Man this day
Hath nowhere his head to rest.

THIEF ON LEFT.

If thou be God's son, and free,
Why hang'st thou upon this hill
To save thyself now let us see
And us two that suffer ill.

THIEF ON RIGHT.

Man, trouble him not – be still!
Doest thou thy God fear naught?
We have deserved thus to spill
For all of the evil we wrought
We're come to this.

No ill did he
Thus for to die.
Lord, have mind of me
When thou art come to bliss.

JESUS.

Son, shalt thou be this day with me
In Paradise.

It begins to grow darker.

Eli! Eli!
My God, my God full free
Lama sabacthani?
Why hast thou forsaken me
In care?
Who never did ill –
But be it at thy will
For I will still
Endure
(*To audience*.) Man on mould be meek to me
And have thy maker in thy mind
And think what I have borne for thee
With peerless pains here to be pined.
He who on me in faith relies
Now from his foes shall I defend
And on the third day right uprise
And so to Heaven I shall ascend.
O, Father, hear my boon
For now all things have end
And unto thee right soon
My spirit I commend...
In manus tuas.

MARY.

Alas! See my dear son is slain
And cruelly reft is all my rede
All comfort and kindness is vain
Alas! for my darling, my dear.

JOHN.

Ah, Mother, come, hold up your head
And sigh not with sorrows so sere.

PILATE.
>Sir Longinus. Come here.
>Thrust thy spear –
>No longer bide –
>In Jesu's side.

CENTURION.
>Truly I say
>God's son was he
>And slain today
>Unworthily.

PILATE.
>Joseph of Arimathea – welcome are ye to me
>Say friend, what would you have?

JOSEPH OF ARIMATHEA.
>Give me then Jesus' body – Lord Pilate I beg thee
>To anoint and lay in grave.

PILATE.
>With all my heart then, lay him gently to rest.
>I grant thy request.

>*Descent from the cross:* LONGINUS, CENTURION,
>JOSEPH, NICODEMUS, *etc*.

NICODEMUS.
>Let all mankind mark in his mind
>This sorrowful sight for all to see
>No falseness in him could they find
>That slew our lord sans all mercy.

JOSEPH.
>A grave have I
>And by and by
>There shall he lie
>In linen cloths wound.

NICODEMUS.
>Our friend was he
>Faithful and free
>Therefore go we
>To grave him in ground.

38. The Carpenters

Soliloquy.

CENTURION
> To maintain truth is well worthy.
> I told you when I saw him die
> That he was God's Son Almighty
> That hangeth there.
> Still say I so, and stand thereby
> For evermore.
>
> The Sun for woe he waxed all wan
> The Moon and stars denied to shine
> The Earth itself in sorrow shook –
> Weeping for his sake.
> The stones that never stirred ere then
> Asunder break.
>
> All that I tell, for truth should ye
> Evermore trust.
> For this same death ye all did work –
> Say how the veil rent in your kirk
> And why Sun, Moon, and stars grew dark
> Explain to me.
> God grant ye grace that ye may know
> The truth some day.

> *At the tomb.*

FIRST SOLDIER.
> Now men, ye know, we are all bound
> To keep his body safe in't ground.
> Let each man here then sit him down
> And guard this tomb.

THIRD SOLDIER.
> And any thief that snoops around
> We'll crack his crown.

> *They fall into a deep sleep. Sun rises.*

MARY.
> Alas! Who shall assuage my grief
> When think I on his wounds that bled
> Jesu, my son of love most sweet,

High on that hill?
He's dead and graven under grit
Who ne'er did ill.

MARY TWO.

Since he is slain, my sisters dear,
Wend we now all three together
With our ointments fair and clear
That we have brought
To 'noint his wounds on sides sere
That men him wrought.

MARY THREE.

Go we along, my sisters free,
Full fair us longs his corse to see.
But I wot not how best may be –
Help have we none –
And who shall here among us three
Remove the stone.

MARY TWO.

Though we were more, we may not do,
For it is huge and heavy too.

MARY THREE.

Sisters, look here – come, look inside
The heavy stone is rolled away...
Now let us wend
To bathe our lord, and with him stay,
That was our friend.

GABRIEL.

Ye mourning women, lost in thought
Here in this place whom have ye sought?

MARY.

My son, that unto death was brought –
Young man, say where is he?

GABRIEL.

Woman, be sure, here he is not.
Come and see.
He is not here, the sooth to say
The place is void where once he lay
The linen cloth here may you see

Was on him laid.
But he is risen and gone his way
As he hath said –
Risen through the Father's mastery.

To his disciples wend ye now
He must be sought in Galilee
Go – tell them so.

GABRIEL *disappears*. *Exeunt* MARYS. *Music wakes*
SOLDIERS.

THIRD SOLDIER.
What! Out alas! What can I say! –
Where is the corse that herein lay?

FIRST SOLDIER.
What ails thee, lad? Is he away
That we should tent?

THIRD SOLDIER.
Get up and see –

SECOND SOLDIER.
Ah weladay! –

THIRD SOLDIER.
We'll all be shent!

FOURTH SOLDIER *enters*.

FOURTH SOLDIER.
What the devil is this? What ails you, men
Such noise and racket must ye make?

THIRD SOLDIER.
Alack, he's gone!

FOURTH SOLDIER.
What! Him in't tomb?

SECOND SOLDIER.
Yea, look here where he lay.

FOURTH SOLDIER.
Ha, harrow! Devils! How'd'ee get away?
If once Sir Pilate wit this deed

That we were sleeping when he fleed
We will forfeit – mark my word –
All that we have.

FIRST SOLDIER.
Us must tell lies, for there is need
Ourselves to save.

SECOND SOLDIER.
I say so too – we'll give it a go.

FOURTH SOLDIER.
And I shall back your lies also.

FIRST SOLDIER.
An hundred, shall I say, and mo'
Armed to the teeth each one
Did steal away his corse – although
We were all near slain.

THIRD SOLDIER.
Not me. I say there's nought to do
But tell the truth e'en as it happed
And how he rose, and me and you –
And death too – he 'scaped.

SECOND SOLDIER.
What – dare thou to Sir Pilate go
With these ill tidings and tell him so?

THIRD SOLDIER.
I dare. And if he slay us too
We die but once.

FOURTH SOLDIER.
Go we then to make or mend
We must now to Sir Pilate wend
I fear he and we shall not part friends…
Let's hence.

39. Winedrawers

Enter MARY MAGDALENE *distraught and weeping*.

JESUS.
>Thou woman wandering in the way
>Whom do ye seek this livelong day?

MAGDALENE.
>Jesus my Lord I seek alway
>Who for my sins did sorely bleed.
>Sweet sir, if thou hast born him away
>Tell me at once and there me lead
>Where thou him hid –

MARY.
>Mary.

MAGDALENE.
>Ah! Rabboni! I have thee sought –

JESUS.
>Away, and Mary, touch me not
>But take good heart from what I say.
>Unto our God, my Father dear
>Now – in due time I shall ascend
>For now I may not long dwell here.
>I have accomplished all he did intend.
>And therefore learn, all ye who hear,
>How all on Earth their lives must mend
>To all that love me I draw near
>To bring them in bliss withouten end.
>
>To Galilee now shalt thou wend,
>Magdalen, my daughter dear
>My brethren there for me attend
>My blessing on thee and all these here.

42. Sciveners

PETER.
>Alas! To woe now we are brought!
>Never had men so mickle thought
>Since that our Lord to death was brought
>On Calvary hill.

JAMES.
>Out of this place durst go we not
>But here must dwell.

JOHN.
>For since our foes wrought us that wrong
>Our Lord to slay
>Them we dare never come among
>Nor flee away.

>JESUS *appears in a beam of light then disappears.*

>Ah! Brethren dear, what may we trow –
>What was this sight that we saw now
>Shining so bright?

JAMES.
>It vanished thus – who can say how? –
>Out of our sight.

JOHN.
>It troubles me – What light it brought!

PETER.
>What e'er it be – and to my thought –
>'Twas vanity –

JESUS.
>   Peace be with you – and ever may it be,
>Be nought afraid for I am he.

PETER.
>In God's name, *benedicite*!
>What may this mean?

JAMES.
>It is a spirit – and not he –
>That we have seen.

JESUS.

> I am the Christ and fear ye nought.
> Here may ye see...
> My body that mankind hath bought
> Upon the tree.
> In flesh I come among you straight
> Behold and touch my hands and feet
> And closely clasp these wound still wet
> Believe in me.

THOMAS *approaches the room.*

THOMAS.

> Unto my brethren I will wend –
> In fear they dwell.
> All hope of bliss there's never none
> Our joy and succour is all gone
> Of nothing but mourning we hear the sound
> In all this land.
> God bless us brethren blood and bone
> On every hand.

PETER.

> Now welcome, Thomas. Where has thou been?
> Jesus in flesh we here have seen
> On ground to go.

THOMAS.

> What say ye, men? Your wits, I ween,
> Are lost for woe.

JOHN.

> Sure, Thomas, true, we do not feign
> Jesus our friend is risen again –

THOMAS.

> Speak not to me – these hopes are vain
> He that was late and foully slain?
> How could he rise? Poor men ye dream –

JOHN.

> Nay, Thomas, nay, if thou hads't seen –

THOMAS.

> Cease to persuade – prithee no more –

Until I see his body bare
And touch the wound the spear did shear
Ne'er shall I trow these tales, I wean.

JOHN.

Thomas that wound we all have seen –

THOMAS.

Never! Ye know not what ye mean! –
Or wits ye want.
Unkind to me that cause me pain
With tricks to taunt.

JESUS.

Peace brethren, now be unto you
And Thomas, attend to what I say.
Put forth thy fingers to me now
These hands – dost see? –
Here for man's bliss were nailèd through
Upon the tree.

THOMAS.

My Lord, my God – full well I see!
Ah, precious blood, blest might thou be!
Mankind on Earth, behold and see...
Mercy, my God, I beg of thee.

JESUS.

Thomas, since thou hast seen this sight
Ye do believe it. But every wight –
Blest be he ever –
That trusts in my resurrection right
But saw it never.

43. Tailors

ANGELS *gather and sing*.

JESUS.
Now is my way in world at end
My time that here on Earth was lent
Unto my Father I now ascend –
Your Father too – who first me sent.
My God, your God, and each man's friend
That will unto His word attend.
Sin's power on Earth hath here an end
If Man repents and will make mend.
My Father's work fulfilled have I
Therefore, farewell, to ye I say
I shall prepare a place for ye
Where you shall dwell with me for aye.
Father, receive me in bliss on high
Now I ascend and come to thee
His blessing here I leave with ye...
Ascendo ad patrem meum.

He ascends into Heaven. [*Or up into the Minster roof and
out through the trap.*]

48. Mercers

GOD THE FATHER.
Angels, ring out your clarions clear
Summon all creatures here to me
Learnèd and unlettered – man and wife –
Receive their dooms of me shall they –
Yea – every one that ere had life –
None be forgotten – nor great, nor small –
They shall survey those wounds five
My son hath suffered for them all.
Sunder ye them – here in my sight –
Equal in bliss they shall not be
My blessed children, in glorious light,
On my right hand I shall them see.
And soon shall every wicked wight

From my left hand in terror flee.
This day, these dooms shall I indite
To each man... as he hath servèd me.

MICHAEL.

Loved be Thou Lord, in might the most.
That angels serve as messengers.
Thy will shall be obeyed in haste
That Heaven, and Earth, and Hell shall hear.

Single trumpet call. Exit GOD.

Good, ill, and each and ilka ghost
Rise in the flesh ye once did wear
For words and worlds wend all to waste
Draw to your doom – your end is near.

GABRIEL.

Ilka creature, both eld and young
Come from your graves – we bid ye rise!
Body and soul I bid ye bring
And stand before the great assize
For I am sent from Heaven's King
Some Him to bless, but more chastise.
Therefore rise up and give reckoning!

All the ANGELS *blow their trumpets for a long time...*
LUCIFER *enters with his* DEVILS.

LUCIFER.

What the devil's going on?
I bad ye should be boun
If that Jesus disturbed us mo'
That you should ding him down
And beat him black and blue.

BELZEBUB.

Say? – 'black and blue' – that's easy for you
Come yourself and have a go
None may abide his bitter blow
He'll maul and mar us all the mo'.

LUCIFER.

Fainthearts! What are ye all scared?
Haven't ye the strength to flit him fro?

See quick that all my gear's prepared
Myself shall to the gadling go.

LUCIFER *puts on armour, takes a weapon, and*
approaches MICHAEL.

Stop there – my friend – stand still
Cease all thy bluster there,
And tell me if you will
What the hell are you doing down here?

JESUS.
(*Appearing as Christ the King*.)
Michael, my angel, come to me
Drive out yon demons – chase them away.
And that false Lucifer, cast him I say
Into flames for all eternity.

Trumpets: MICHAEL, *etc., drive* DEVILS *back into Hell*.

LUCIFER.
Out! Wheee! Harrow! Help, Mahoun!
Now wax I wood out of my wit!

BELZEBUB.
Well what did you expect? I knew this would happen.
We told you what would come of it!

LUCIFER.
It's not fair! You've not seen the last of me –

DEVILS *suddenly cut off. Trumpets. The dead begin to rise*
up and assemble including all the characters in the play –
good and bad.

BEADLE.
Ah! Loved be thou, Lord of all
That Heaven and Earth and all hast wrought
That at thine angels' trumpet call
Out from our graves we here are brought.

MALCHUS.
Alack! Now wakens my worsest fear
Our wicked ways we may not hide
But on our backs we must them bear –
Alas! We must this day abide!

MICHAEL *separates* GOOD *and* EVIL SOULS *with his flaming sword.*

MICHAEL.
Stand not together – part you in twain.
Ye shall not be all one in bliss.
The Father in Heaven doth so ordain,
For many of ye have wrought amiss.

The DEVILS *peep nervously out of Hell.*

LUCIFER.
Fellows this is a wondrous sight!
Stoke up the fires, heat up your tongs –
For if that Doomsman deal aright
We'll welcome in a goodly throng.

JESUS.
Now every soul to me attend,
Judgement upon you all I bring
This world of woe away is went
And I am come a crownèd king.
The Father in Heaven hath sent me down
To doom your deeds and make an end.
Judgement Day on you is come
Answer, as ye shall your souls defend.
Surely, surely, ye ought to quake,
This dreadful day, this sight to see –
All this I suffered for thy sake,
Say, man, what suffered thou for me?
My children blest on my right hand
Your doom this day ye need not dread
For all your comfort I command –
Your life in liking shall ye lead.
When I was hungry, ye me fed
To slake my thirst your heart was free
When I was naked, ye me clad
Ye would no sorrow upon me see.
When in prison I was stead
Of my pain ye had pity.
Or sick – when I was brought to bed
Kindly ye came to comfort me.

BEADLE.

> Maker Almighty, when had we
> Or meat or drink, thy want to feed?

ANOTHER GOOD SOUL.

> When was it we brought clothes to thee? –
> Or visited thee in any need?

JESUS.

> When *any* had need, through night and day
> Or asked for help you gave it free
> Your good hearts never said them nay
> That love you gave came unto me.

> *To the* BAD SOULS.

> When I had need of drink or meat,
> Caitiffs, ye drave me from your gate –
> I stood without, weary and wet
> While ye smiled down like lords in state.
> When I was sick and sorriest
> Ye tended me not – for I was poor
> In prison cast in chains and fast
> None of you cared what pains I bore.
> When I could find no place to rest
> With blows you drove me from your door.
> Oft when I shivering was and cold
> For all you cared I naked went
> House nor harbour, help nor hold,
> Although I begged ye never lent.
> Miseries on me were manifold
> But none of you my sorrows slaked –
> Ye all forsook me, young and old…
> Therefore, shall I now ye forsake.

MALCHUS.

> When had ye, Lord, that doth all possess
> Hunger or thirst, since God thou art –
> When was't that thou in prison was
> When saw we thee naked or harbourless?

ANOTHER BAD SOUL.

> When did we this unkindness!

YET ANOTHER BAD SOUL.
When did we so much wickedness!

JESUS.
Caitiffs, as oft as it betid
The needy asked aught in my name
Ye heard them not, your ears ye shut,
Your charity was not at home –
To me was that unkindness shown.
Therefore ye bear this bitter blame
To least or most when ye it did
To me ye did the self and same.
My chosen children come unto me
With me to dwell now shall ye wend
Where joy and bliss shall ever be
Your life in liking shall ye spend.
Ye cursèd caitiffs flee from me
In Hell to pine withouten end
Ye shall know nought but misery
Subjects of Lucifer, the fiend.

The ANGELS *drive the* BAD SOULS *to Hell.*

GOD.
Now is fulfilled all my forethought
For ended is all earthly thing
All upon Earth that I have wrought
After their deeds have deserving.
They that would sin and cease for nought
Of sorrows sere now shall they sing,
But all that mended them while they might
Shall dwell for aye with my blessing.

And thus he maketh an end, with melody of ANGELS
crossing from place to place.

Glossary

aux armes – to arms
aye (1) – yes
aye (2) – always, continually, ever
bairn – child
boun – make ready, prepare
brent– burnt
caitiff – a base, cowardly, or despicable person
corse – corpse
dight – to dress, adorn, equip
ding – to strike, knock down
dole – sorrow, grief, dolor
eke – also
eld – old age
fain – gladly
hale – draw or drag forcefully
ilka – every, each
iwis – certainly, assuredly
ken/kenned – know/known
liefer – gladly, willingly
losel – a worthless person
lour – look angry or sullen, scowl
lurdan – an idle or incompetent person
malison – curse
mickle – a large amount
mun – must
quean – woman; prostitute
rede – to give counsel to; advise, explain
sere – dry or withered
shent – ruined, destroyed; put to shame
skelp – strike, slap, or smack
swink – labour, toil
tite – immediate
trashes – ragged clothes

weal – well-being, prosperity, or happiness; wealth or riches
ween – believe
weladay/welaway – alas
wight – creature; being, human being
wot – know

A Nick Hern

This version of *The York Mystery Plays* first published in Great Britain as a paperback original in 2016 by Nick Hern Books Limited, The Glasshouse, 49a Goldhawk Road, London W12 8QP

The York Mystery Plays copyright © 2016 Mike Poulton

Mike Poulton has asserted his right to be identified as the author of this version

Cover image by Sally Walker
Designed and typeset by Nick Hern Books, London
Printed in Great Britain by CPI Group (UK) Ltd

A CIP catalogue record for this book is available from the British Library

ISBN 978 1 84842 538 5